Showcase 500 rings

Showcase 500 rings

New Directions in Art Jewelry

Bruce Metcalf, Juror

LARK
CRAFTS
Asheville

SENIOR EDITOR
Marthe Le Van

EDITOR
Julie Hale

ART DIRECTOR
Kathleen Holmes

ART PRODUCTION
Matt Shay

COVER DESIGNER
Chris Bryant

FRONT COVER,
CLOCKWISE FROM MAIN IMAGE
Isabelle Posillico
Aqua Satellite, 2006

Serin Oh
Imitation & Deception, 2011

Chris Ploof
Mokume Gane Hollow-Construction Ring with Chalcedony, 2010

Catalina Brenes
El, 2009

BACK COVER,
CLOCKWISE FROM TOP LEFT
Terhi Tolvanen
Bleu, 2010

Cinnamon Lee
Hidden Love, 2010

Ben Neubauer
Square Ring, 2009

Yong Joo Kim
Reconfiguring the Ordinary: Lassoed and Overlapped, 2011

Liaung Chung Yen
Blossom Ring, 2007

SPINE
Elena Thiveou
Cyclop, 2010

FRONT FLAP
Ralph Bakker
Solitaire 1, 2008

BACK FLAP
Fabrizio Tridenti
Restricted Area, 2010

TITLE PAGE
Sharon Vaizer
My Little Fun Ta Sea, 2011

OPPOSITE
Maria Cristina Bellucci
11 Ring 4, 2011

LARK CRAFTS

An Imprint of Sterling Publishing
387 Park Avenue South
New York, NY 10016

If you have questions or comments
about this book, please visit: larkcrafts.com

Library of Congress Cataloging-in-Publication Data

Le Van, Marthe.
  Showcase 500 rings : new directions in art jewelry / Marthe Le Van. — 1st ed.
     p. cm.
  ISBN 978-1-4547-0288-7
  1. Rings. I. Title. II. Title: Showcase five hundred rings.
  NK7444.L48 2012
    739.27'82—dc23
            2011036673

10 9 8 7 6 5 4 3 2 1

First Edition

Published by Lark Crafts
An Imprint of Sterling Publishing Co., Inc.
387 Park Avenue South, New York, NY 10016

Distributed in Canada by Sterling Publishing,
c/o Canadian Manda Group, 165 Dufferin Street
Toronto, Ontario, Canada M6K 3H6

Distributed in the United Kingdom by GMC Distribution Services,
Castle Place, 166 High Street, Lewes, East Sussex, England BN7 1XU

Distributed in Australia by Capricorn Link (Australia) Pty Ltd.,
P.O. Box 704, Windsor, NSW 2756 Australia

ISBN 13: 978-1-4547-0288-7

For information about custom editions, special sales, and premium and corporate purchases, please contact the Sterling Special Sales Department at 800-805-5489 or specialsales@sterlingpub.com.

Requests for information about desk and examination copies available to college and university professors must be submitted to academic@larkbooks.com. Our complete policy can be found at www.larkcrafts.com.

contents

introduction

Imagine you're a jeweler, and you want to make a ring. And suppose you don't want to reproduce an existing ring. You want to do something different. The creative jeweler will consider the ring and its long history, and ask, "What else can I do?" This book is full of "what else," which is why it is quite magical. You'll find the unexpected and the visionary. You'll see creativity in action. It's a trip, as we used to say.

Having looked at nearly 6,500 images of rings, I'm pleased to report that studio jewelry is healthy, vibrant, and pluralistic. No single aesthetic dominates the field today: a number of approaches jostle for attention. Many rings feature gold and gems and show a continuing fascination with real, seductive beauty in a contemporary voice. There is a pervasive interest in clunky forms and crusty surfaces. Alternative materials abound. For those concerned about de-skilling, I found the average level of workmanship to be reassuringly good.

Of all the current trends, I find the clunky/crusty one to be the most fascinating. Relaxed craftsmanship, awkward forms, and randomly textured surfaces have been part of studio jewelry since the field emerged in the late 19th century. Madeline Yale Wynne, the first recorded American studio jeweler, had very little skill—and didn't care in the least. Forty years later, Alexander Calder banged out jewelry with a hammer and a pair of pliers and changed the history of the field. Around the same time, Sam Kramer melted blobs of metal together to wonderful effect. Traditional standards of tradecraft were not incorporated into studio jewelry until the emergence of artists like John Paul Miller, who came to prominence in the 1950s. A certain tension has remained between high and low craftsmanship ever since.

In the fine arts, clunk can be traced back to sculptor Jean Dubuffet in the late 1940s; to the highly textured surfaces deployed by Abstract Expressionist sculptors like Herbert Ferber and Theodore Roszak; and to all the actions and interventions of the late 1950s and 1960s, from the Arte Povera movement to sculptor Claes Oldenburg. Clunk was a critical response to conventional sculpture, especially polished bronze and marble. Inelegant forms stood in opposition to the outmoded idea that art must be beautiful. Instead, it was proposed that art should be interesting.

In many ways, clunk is a critique of conventional preciousness. Today, Karl Fritsch is the king of clunk jewelry. Fritsch's unrefined castings and funky stone settings are designed, in part, to correct the unimaginative tradecraft to which every young German jeweler is apprenticed. The disciplines of tradecraft are inverted. Trade jewelers insist on absolutely resolved forms and lovely finishes. Fritsch and his many followers insist on irregular forms and rude surfaces.

I get the feeling that crust and clunk are still regarded by a large number of studio jewelers as having an avant-garde status within the field. Serious young jewelers reject the moral strictures of the trade and seek out their opposite. But crust and clunk are not avant-garde, unless you propose that jewelry exists in its own little world, utterly divorced from all developments in the fine arts, design, and other crafts. In fact, studio jewelry remains highly blinkered, sometimes unaware of much of the rest of the world.

The most blinkered genre in studio jewelry is gold and gems. The jewelry is often beautiful, expertly crafted, and hyperconservative. Even asymmetry is uncommon in gold and gems, and influences from beyond the confines of the genre

are rarely seen. I note a common dependence on convention that allows growth and change in only the tiniest increments.

On a more positive note, I'm pleased to report forward progress in the areas of digital design and rapid prototyping, both of which are finally infiltrating the world of rings. For years, digitally based jewelry tended toward overlarge extravaganzas. But now, as digital design skills proliferate and rapid prototyping materials continuously improve, a new generation of jewelers is dispensing with giganticism and turning toward realistic forms of jewelry in sizes that might actually be worn. As far as I'm concerned, this shift counts as forward progress.

In jurying the book, a few other trends and some notable individual contributions caught my attention. Four or five rings made of human teeth were submitted for consideration. I can think of no reason why teeth should be the art supply du jour, but there it is. I also noticed a lot of black jewelry, which I'm beginning to find just as reflexive and unimaginative as polished metal was 40 years ago. What's with all the Calvinist severity?

I was thrilled to see pure kitsch appropriated by Märta Mattsson in *White Vader* (page 272). This delightfully sarcastic pink and white ring is a standout. So is Yong Joo Kim's *Reconfiguring the Ordinary: Lassoed and Overlapped* on page 21, which uses an ordinary material—hook-and-loop tape—in a surprising way. Every once in a while, I came across a ring that challenged me, including Limor Leshinsker's ring made of a roll of packing tape with a stone set in it (page 372).

There are a fair number of rings in multiples, which I enjoy. Serial production takes the emphasis away from preciousness and obsessive craftsmanship, forcing the observer to look at variations rather than individual compositions. Of all the multiples, Julie Usel's rings made of carved and dyed potatoes (page 247) jump out. Now, that is memorable!

This book is a celebration of the imagination. Look at the wild variety of work we've included, the extremes of artistic approaches. There's no dominant style here, and that's a good thing. The collection is highly individualistic. It comes from all over the world. It is testimony to the incredible energy and spirit of experimentation in the studio jewelry world. I hope you enjoy this collection!

Bruce Metcalf, Juror

BRUCE METCALF
Claw Ring ■ 2011
4.5 x 6.2 cm
Sterling silver, Micarta, painted composite cork
PHOTO BY ARTIST

DOUG BUCCI
Natalya ■ 2010
2.8 x 2.2 x 0.8 cm
18-karat gold, diamonds; 3D printed
PHOTO BY KEN YANOVIAK

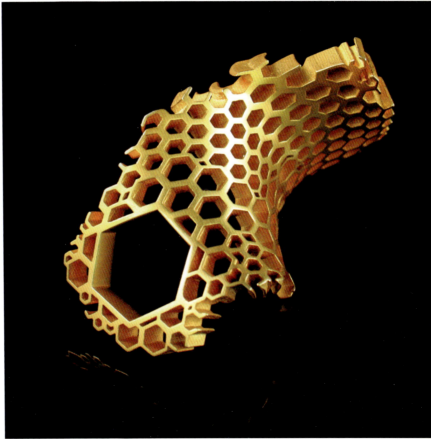

KAROLINA BIK
Honeycomb Ring ■ 2009
7 x 2.8 x 0.6 cm
Sterling silver, 22-karat gold plate; CAD,
rapid prototyped, cast, sandblasted
PHOTOS BY ARTIST

9

RALPH BAKKER
Solitaire 1 ■ 2008
5 x 2.5 x 2.5 cm
Gold, silver, enamel, lemon quartz
PHOTO BY MICHAEL ANHALT

FACING PAGE
TODD REED
Raw Diamond Cube Rings ■ 2011
Largest: 2.5 x 2.5 x 3.5 cm
Silver, raw diamond, patina
PHOTO BY CRAIG PRATT

MICHA YEHIELI
Untitled ■ 2008

4.9 x 2.3 x 1.6 cm
Fine silver; forged
PHOTO BY ALEXANDER KUCHERENKO

JIEUN PARK
Human + Ring—3 (Group) ■ 2006
12 x 3.5 x 14.5 cm
Copper, patina
PHOTO BY MYOUNG WOOK HUH

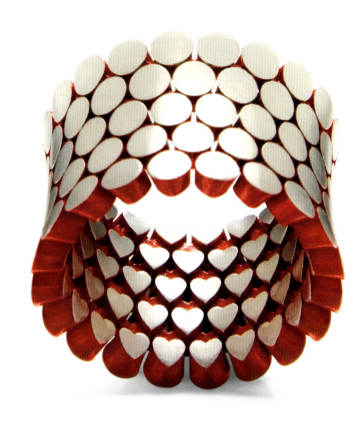

FACING PAGE
CHRISTEL VAN DER LAAN
Wholeheartedly ■ 2011
3.8 x 3.7 x 3.1 cm
Ceramic honeycomb block, 18-karat
gold; carved, painted, fabricated
PHOTO BY ADRIAN LAMBERT

CINNAMON LEE
Hidden Love ■ 2010
1.2 x 2.4 x 2.4 cm
Sterling silver, cold enamel; 3D modeled,
rapid prototyped, cast, hand painted
PHOTO BY FRANCES MOCNIK

15

FABRIZIO TRIDENTI
Untitled ◼ 2010
5.8 x 4.3 x 3.4 cm
Brass, acrylic paint, enamel; constructed
PHOTO BY ARTIST

MARJORIE SCHICK
Orbiting Rings: Balancing Act ■ 2004
Largest ring: 6.4 x 4.4 x 1.9 cm
Wood; cut, constructed, carved, painted
PHOTOS BY GARY POLLMILLER

LAWRENCE WOODFORD
Blossom ▪ 2006
3 x 2.5 x 2.5 cm
Sterling silver; fabricated
PHOTO BY PAUL FOURNIER

YAEL HERMAN
Zebra Crushed Ring ■ 2010
3 x 3 x 2 cm
Silver, palladium; handmade, crushed
PHOTO BY NATAN DVIR

ANASTASIA KANDARAKI
Parla Piu Forte ■ 2010

5 x 4 x 1.5 cm
Sterling silver; oxidized
PHOTO BY FEDERICO CAVICCHIOLI

YONG JOO KIM
Reconfiguring the Ordinary:
Lassoed and Overlapped ■ 2011

8 x 8 x 2 cm
Hook-and-loop tape; fabricated
PHOTO BY AFFANDI SETIAWAN

21

IAN HENDERSON
Tchaikovsky ■ 2010

8 x 5 x 3 cm
Aluminum grounding wire, synthetic rubber
insulation tubing; forged, cut, layered, heat treated
PHOTO BY TOM BLOOM

MEGAN DUNN
Untitled ■ 2004
6.5 x 5.5 x 4 cm
Sterling silver; fabricated
PHOTO BY ROBERT DIAMANTE

Inspiration for this ring came from my observation of the fragile lines of fingerprints. When it came to choosing a material, titanium, which is hard and durable yet light and ethereal, was a natural choice. —SL

STEFANIA LUCCHETTA
Digital 13 Ring ■ 2010
3 x 4.5 x 4 cm
Titanium; rapid prototyped, hand polished
PHOTOS BY ARTIST

I create pieces of jewelry by means of three forces: kinetic energy, represented by high pressure; thermal energy; and the cohesive strength of metal. The archaic character of my work lies in the material itself—iron or steel—and in the dark coloration of the surfaces. The work then undergoes transformation through fire, a process that changes a static, geometric solid into something biomorphic and filled with energy. —AA

ALIKI APOUSSIDOU
Siegelring Rund ■ 2008
2.6 x 2.4 x 1.5 cm
Mild steel; hot forged
PHOTO BY ARTIST

25

Each of these rings is attached to a single sheet of sterling silver or stainless steel. To wear, simply remove a ring from its sheet, file it down, and polish away any rough edges. Once all the rings have been removed, the sheets can be used as decorative wall art or attached to a chain to make a necklace. —AMT

ALISSIA MELKA-TEICHROEW
Ring a Day (Set of Seven Rings) ■ 2005
7 x 28 x 0.1 cm
Sterling silver, stainless steel; photo etched
PHOTOS BY LISA KLAPPE

CATALINA BRENES
El ■ 2009
3.6 x 3.5 x 1 cm
Silver, 24-karat gold,
onyx, resin; handmade
PHOTO BY FEDERICO CAVICCHIOLI

GABRIELA HORVAT
Inner Parts ■ 2010
5 x 4 x 2 cm
Sterling silver, silk, wool; coiled, soldered
PHOTO BY ARTIST

JOANNE WARDROP
Untitled ■ 2011

6.8 x 6.8 x 1.9 cm
Sterling silver, fine silver,
18-karat gold; oxidized
PHOTO BY ARTIST

SHARON VAIZER
my little fun ta sea ■ 2011
10 x 9 x 6 cm
Silk, nylon restraints, Swarovski
crystals; welded, inlaid
PHOTO BY HEFTSY ELGAR

KIM VICTORIA WEARNE
Decay Rings ■ 2007
11 x 14.5 x 9.2 cm
Sterling silver, fine silver, brass, concrete, onyx,
pearls, acrylic paint; fabricated, saw pierced, cast
PHOTO BY ARTIST

ZHAO LI
Finding Neverland ■ 2010
6 x 4.5 x 5.5 cm
Silver, textile, medical-grade plastic
PHOTO BY ARTIST

STEFANIE KÖLBEL
Striped Rings ■ 2008

Largest: 1.3 x 1.6 x 1.6 cm
Stainless steel, polyamide, antique glass beads;
traditional bobbin lace technique, hand dyed
PHOTO BY CLAUDIA GALLWITZ

SHARONA MUIR
Akea Ring ■ 2010
4.5 x 3 x 2.5 cm
Mixed media, citrine, coral, polychrome
PHOTO BY TIM THAYER

MYUNG URSO
Rings—Memory ■ 2010

Left: 2 x 7.5 x 4.5 cm; middle: 4.5 x 5.5 x 1.5 cm; right: 5.6 x 7.5 x 3.2 cm
Silk, oriental ink, thread, sterling silver, lacquer; calligraphy, sewn, forged, oxidized
PHOTO BY TIMOTHY J. FUSS

BURCU BÜYÜKÜNAL
Brilliant ■ 2011
2.5 x 2 x 0.5 cm
14-karat gold, sterling silver; fabricated, oxidized
PHOTO BY ARTIST

CONSTANTINOS KYRIACOU
Can't Follow My Vanity ▪ 2010
10 x 5 x 4.5 cm
Fine silver, fine gold, sterling silver,
acrylic colors; experimental filigree, oxidized

The Tiffany setting engagement ring is a design classic, a symbol of marital bliss. My acrylic diamond rings put a playful spin on the Tiffany tradition. The rings come in various colors, each with a multitude of meanings. In some cultures, yellow signifies jealousy or infidelity, while red symbolizes passion, love, and strength. The rings can be worn individually or in multiples of two or three. —AMT

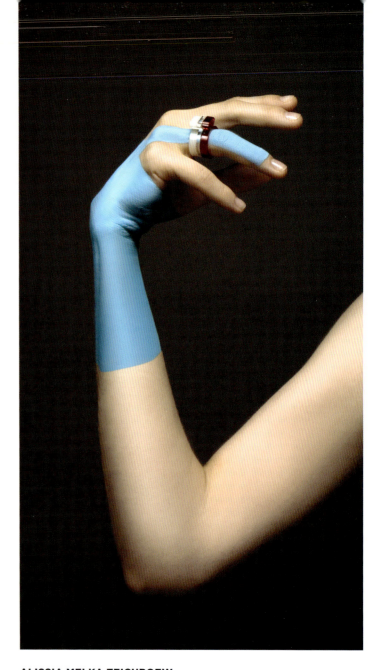

ALISSIA MELKA-TEICHROEW
Diamond Acrylic Rings ■ 2003
Each: 3 x 2.5 x 0.4 cm
Acrylic; laser cut
PHOTOS BY LISA KLAPPE

SALVADOR FRANCISCO NETO
Prisoner ■ 2010
3 x 2.3 x 1.5 cm
18-karat yellow gold, aquamarine,
nylon cable tie; hand fabricated, brushed
PHOTO BY PAULO R. ROCHA

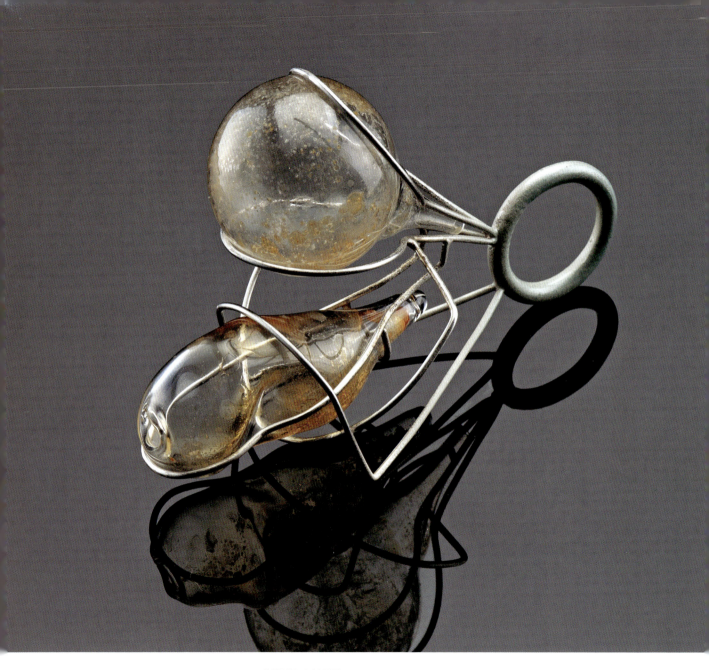

CORAL COHEN
Bactus (The Gray-Blue Ring) ■ 2010
6 x 5 x 3 cm
Sterling silver, glass, bacteria
PHOTO BY AMIT GOSHER

Showcase 500
rings

KEIKO KASHIHARA
Untitled ■ 2010
Each: 2.9 x 2.9 x 0.6 cm
Glass, platinum
PHOTO BY TAKAYUKI SERI

I-HSUAN KUO
The Ring ■ 2011
4 x 3 x 0.5 cm
Copper, enamel
PHOTOS BY ARTIST

GABRIEL CRAIG
Narcissist No. 5 ■ 2008
4.5 x 4.5 x 4.5 cm
Sterling silver, 14-karat gold,
enamel; cast, fabricated
PHOTO BY AMY WEIKS

43

This ring was designed to resemble
Chartres Cathedral. Its top portion spins. —TJC

TZU-JU CHEN
Chartres Cathedral Ring ■ 2005
7.8 x 5 x 3.8 cm
Sterling silver, photographs,
museum boards, tourmalines
PHOTOS BY CHRISTIAN CUTLER

FACING PAGE
HYUNJOO KIM
Play with ■ 2011
Tallest: 15 x 7 x 0.8 cm
Enamel, copper plate; oxidized
PHOTO BY MYOUNG-WOOK HUH

Showcase 500
rings

CALLEY SANCHEZ
Stained Glass Ring 1 ■ 2010
5 x 5 x 2.5 cm
Sterling silver; hand fabricated
PHOTO BY ARTIST

JACQUELINE RYAN
Ring (Moveable Segments) ■ 2009

1.6 cm wide
18-karat gold
PHOTO BY ARTIST

EMANUELA ZAIETTA
Pyramid of Light ■ 2004

3 x 1.5 x 1.3 cm
18-karat gold, rock crystal
PHOTO BY FEDERICO CAVICCHIOLI

SUN LI
Part II ■ 2009
Largest: 2.6 x 2.6 x 0.6 cm
Sterling silver, rhodium plate, sapphires
PHOTO BY STUDIO MUNCH

YOUNG JOO LEE

Moonight, Picture a Scenery III ■ 2009

5 x 5 x 3 cm
Sterling silver, porcelain paint; fabricated
PHOTO BY MYUNG-WOOK HUH

DIANE FALKENHAGEN
Big Pearl Statement Ring I ■ 2007
3.6 x 3.2 x 3.2 cm
Sterling silver, 14-karat gold, glass,
mixed-media image; fabricated
PHOTOS BY BILL POGUE

51

NANCY MELI WALKER
Tassellation ■ 2011
3.7 x 2.1 x 1 cm
22-karat gold, black diamond;
texture milled, fused, fabricated

PHOTO BY CINDY MOMCHILOV

SUSAN SKOCZEN
Gravel and Fight ■ 2006
5.7 x 4.4 x 2.5 cm
Sterling silver, 18-karat gold, pearl, flocking,
acrylic paint; fabricated, oxidized
PHOTO BY DAN FOX

ISABELLE POSILLICO
Aqua Satellite Ring ■ 2010

2.9 x 3.8 x 3.2 cm
18-karat gold, 22-karat gold, aquamarine, diamond,
tourmaline, sapphire; hand fabricated, constructed
PHOTO BY HAP SAKWA

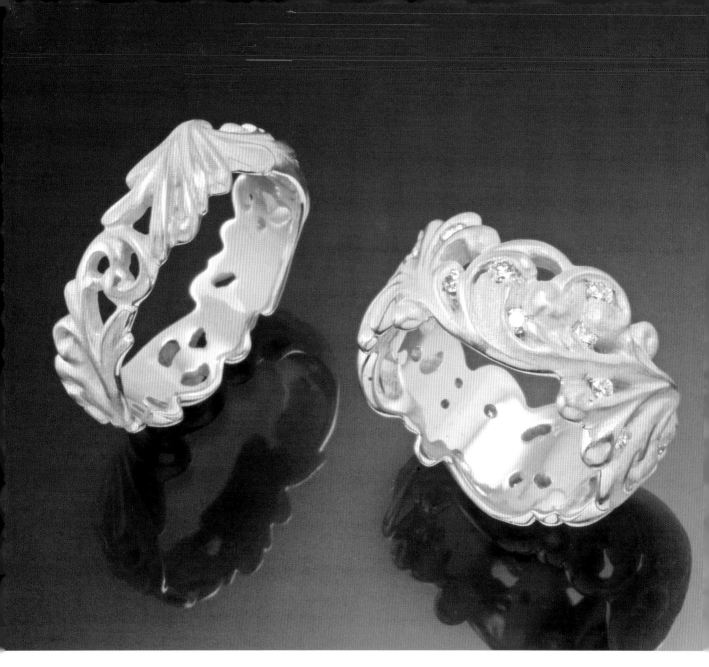

GARRY VANN AUSDLE
Classic Scroll Wedding Set ■ 2010

Each: 1.8 x 1.8 x 1.2 cm
18-karat yellow gold, diamonds; hand carved,
lost wax cast, sandblasted, polished
PHOTO BY PAM PERUGI MARRACCINI

PHILIP SAJET
Á la Recherche du Joyau Perdu ▪ 2011
5.6 x 2 x 2.5 cm
Amethyst, gold, silver, enamel; constructed
PHOTO BY BEATE KLOCKMANN

55

This ring was inspired by the jewelry of ancient Greece, Rome, and Byzantium. The primal approach to artistry brings out the natural beauty of the precious materials. —AK

ANAT KAPLAN
Ancient Treasure ■ 2010
1.5 x 1.9 x 2 cm
14-karat gold, tourmaline, emerald,
aquamarine; hand carved, cast
PHOTO BY JENNA WAKANI

ANDREW NYCE
Catalina-Accented Mokume Diamond Engagement Ring ■ 2010
2.5 x 1.9 x 0.6 cm
18-karat royal yellow gold, 14-karat palladium white gold, palladium-enhanced sterling silver, 14-karat white gold, diamond; diffusion bonded, forged, twisted, patterned, soldered, cast, laser welded
PHOTO BY CHRISTOPHER NYCE

SADIE WANG
Untitled ■ 2009
2.5 x 2.5 x 3.8 cm
Sterling silver and 18-karat gold bimetal, sterling silver, hand-blown glass gem
PHOTO BY AZADPHOTO.COM

ELSA SARANTIDOU
Blossoms ■ 2010
4.5 x 3.2 x 2.5 cm
Sterling silver, 18-karat gold, yellow
diamonds, rhodium plating; sandblasted
PHOTO BY ILIAS PAPAVASILIOU

BETH HYLEN
Breathing Carefully, Detail (Sprout) ◼ 2009
10.2 x 1.3 x 2.5 cm
Silver
PHOTO BY TOMMY ELDER

YOUNGJOO YOO
The Laurel Ring ■ 2010
3.5 x 3.5 x 3.5 cm
18-karat gold and sterling silver bimetal,
sterling silver; hand cut, fabricated
PHOTOS BY STUDIO MUNCH

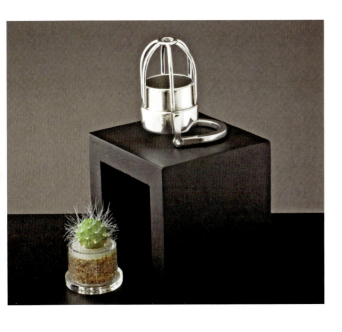

SYLVIE JOUSSET
Catch Me ■ 2010
Height: 4.5 cm
Silver, found cactus; fabricated
PHOTOS BY ANNE-LYSE CHOPIN

LISA BJÖRKE
Untitled ■ 2011
7 x 6 x 4.5 cm
Iron, plaster, model grass,
spray paint; welded, soldered
PHOTO BY MÄRTA MATTSSON

NORA FOK
Artichoke Parachute ■ 2007

12 cm in diameter
Nylon; knotted, woven
PHOTO BY FRANK HILLS

63

ELA BAUER
Untitled ■ 2010

3 cm in diameter
Jade, yarn, metal net, metal
lacquer, silver, mixed media
PHOTOS BY ARTIST

LI-CHU WU
Untitled ■ 2011

3.7 x 4 x 4 cm
Sterling silver, paper; laser cut
PHOTO BY MIKE COLDICOTT AND HSIAO-CHIAO JUAN

BREIT-BAND-DESIGN
Untitled ■ 2008
6.5 x 3.5 x 2.8 cm
Agate geode, polyester
PHOTO BY KATHLEEN TAPLICK

RITA MARCANGELO
Movimento ■ 2009
8 x 7 x 0.5 cm
Silver, silk, acrylic paint; oxidized, burnt
PHOTO BY ADREAN BLOOMARD

KATHERINE JOHANA CORDERO
Soie Emballée ■ 2011

4 x 3.5 x 3 cm
Silk, wool, natural dyes; embroidered, crocheted
PHOTO BY TYLER MACKENZIE

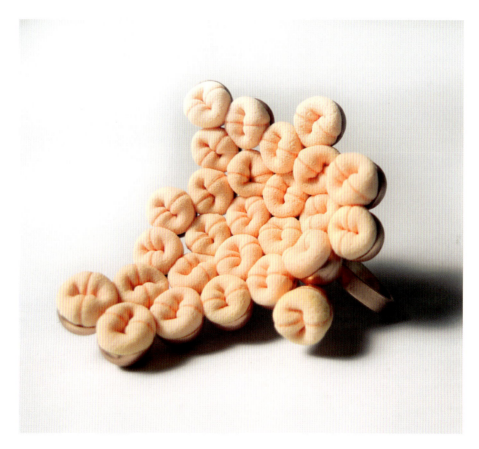

YING-HSIU CHEN
Proliferation II ■ 2011
6.5 x 5.5 x 6 cm
Sterling silver, copper; fabricated
PHOTO BY ARTIST

JESS STARKEL
Hard Candy Rings ▪ 2005

Each: 2.5 x 2.5 x 1.3 cm
Polyurethane rubber, cubic
zirconium, peridot; cast
PHOTO BY ARTIST

RIA LINS
Ring ■ 2009
4 x 3 x 0.7 cm
Wool, textile, embroidery thread, paint, quartz
PHOTO BY DRIES VAN DEN BRANDE

YUN SANGHEE
*Wedding Ring (A Hand That Cannot
Shake Hands)* ■ 2006
7.5 x 12 x 6.5 cm
Asian lacquer, sterling silver, wood, mother-of-pearl
PHOTOS BY STUDIO MUNCH

JO PUDELKO
Untitled ■ 2006
10 x 6.5 x 5.5 cm
Sterling silver, resin; woven, soldered
PHOTO BY ARTIST

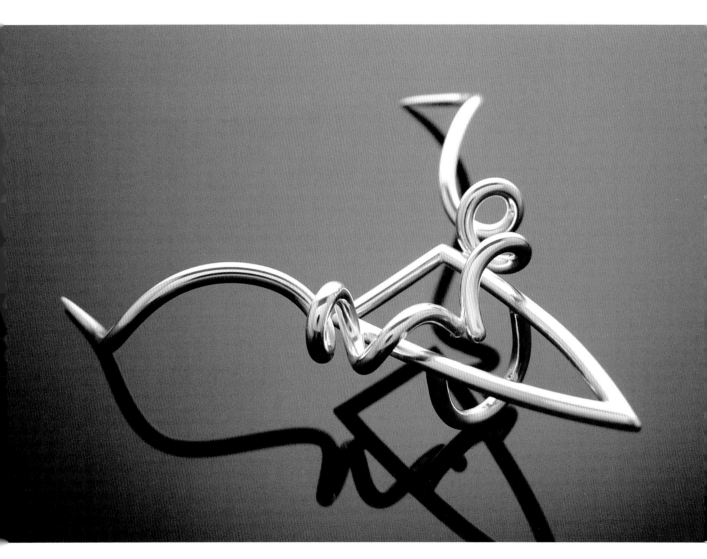

EERO HINTSANEN
Antelope ■ 2007
4 x 13.3 x 12 cm
Sterling silver; constructed, soldered
PHOTO BY CHAO-HSIEN KUO

MANKI KOH
Shooting an Arrow—Kinetic ■ 2009
10 x 8 x 3.5 cm
Sterling silver, spring, magnet, bearing,
bamboo; hand fabricated
PHOTO BY TAESEOK GONG

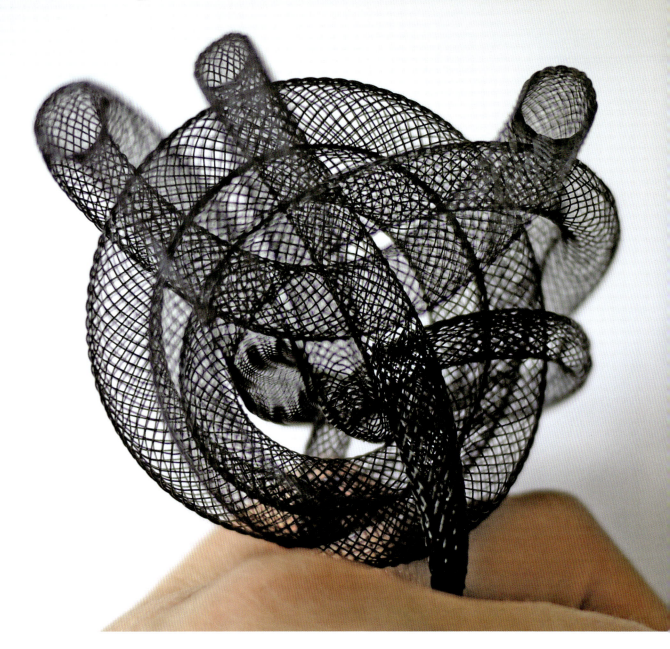

NATALIA GOMENSORO
Maria Ring ■ 2010
7.2 x 5.4 x 4.2 cm
Sterling silver, plastic mesh; assembled
PHOTO BY ARTIST

DIKLA ROZEN
Dancing of the Shadows ■ 2010
12 x 28 x 28 cm
Brass, sterling silver, ostrich feather; oxidized
PHOTO BY JOEY COHEN

DANIEL COOK
Magnetic Wedding Set ■ 2009
Each: 9 x 7 x 3 cm
Silver, iron, magnets; cast
PHOTO BY ARTIST

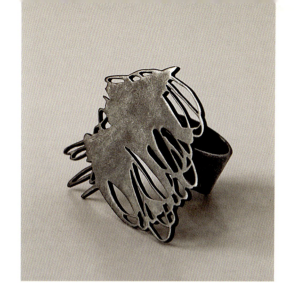

ANNE-MARIE BERNHARDT
Restless ■ 2009
2.7 x 4.8 x 4.2 cm
Sterling silver, paper, graphite;
oxidized, hand fabricated, soldered
PHOTOS BY SOFIA AKERSTEDT

79

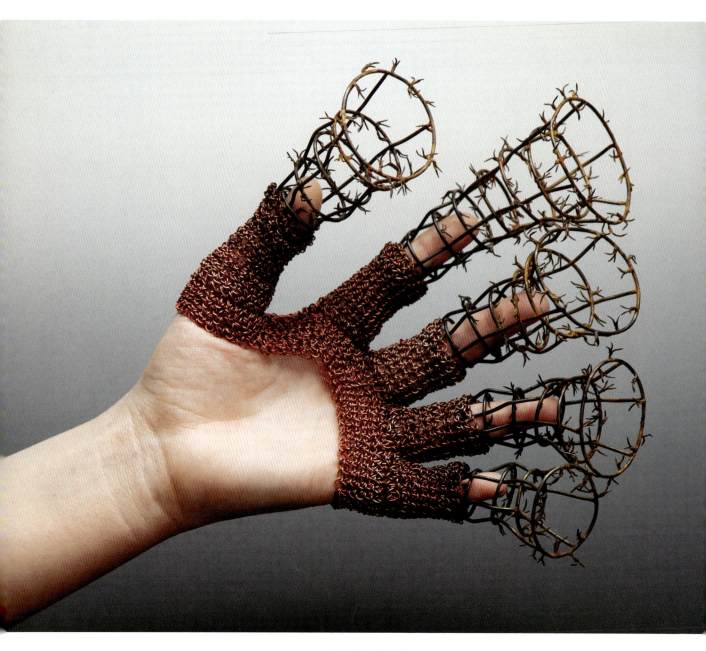

DAMIA SMITH
Defense Mechanism ■ 2011
22.9 x 20.3 x 8.9 cm
Anodized aluminum, steel; crocheted, fused
PHOTO BY BEATRIZ PARRA

KELLY JEAN CONVOY
Passing ■ 2011
6.7 x 3.5 x 2.5 cm
Bone, copper, patina, sterling silver
PHOTO BY ARTIST

MAUREEN BRUSA ZAPPELLINI
Buzz ■ 2010
5 x 4 x 4 cm
Wasp's nest, fine silver; fabricated, assembled
PHOTO BY ARTIST

LUZIA VOGT
Flüchtige Momente ▪ 2006

Various dimensions
Sterling silver, porcelain;
collected, cut, cast
PHOTOS BY ARTIST

YU-JIN LEE
Personating Parrot ■ 2011

9 x 3 x 6.5 cm
Sterling silver, brass, paint, synthetic wood
PHOTO BY SANG-DEOK HAN

ROBERTA WILLIAMSON
DAVID WILLIAMSON

Specimen Collection ■ 2010

14 x 20 x 20 cm
Sterling silver, steel, quartz crystal, antique paper, tin, glass, moss;
fabricated, formed, bezel set, oxidized, carved, lost wax cast, cut

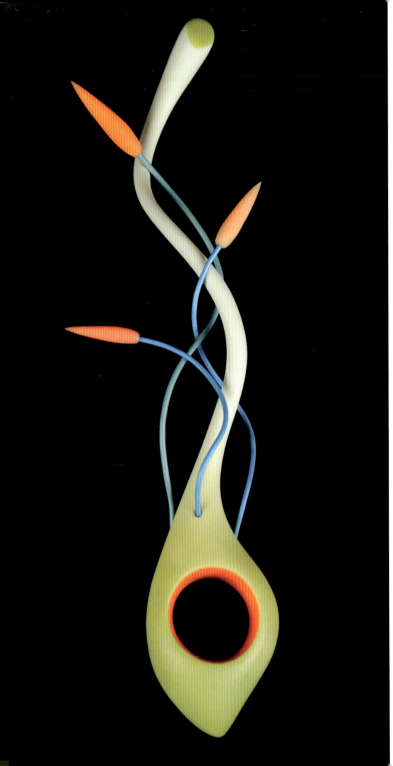

All my work, regardless of scale, is sculptural in nature. *Rise—The Promise of Spring* is an entirely new form for me. I love the notion of a portable sculpture that's always at one's fingertips. That idea supersedes any constraints of functionality the ring may have. **—JLD**

JEFFREY LLOYD DEVER
Rise: The Promise of Spring ■ 2011
17.8 x 5.1 x 2.5 cm
Polymer clay, reclaimed paper clips, steel wire, cardstock; fabricated, sculpted, assembled
PHOTO BY GREGORY R. STALEY

JILLIAN PALONE
Nestle ■ 2010
Largest: 8.8 x 4.4 x 6.3 cm
Paper clay, paint, colored pencils; hand built
PHOTO BY ANNIE PENNINGTON

ELENA THIVEOU
Cyclop ■ 2010
3.8 x 1.9 x 1.6 cm
18-karat gold, blue topaz
PHOTO BY ALEXANDER CROWE

ANDRZEJ BOSS
Rings ■ 2005
Largest: 5.8 x 4.8 x 3.6 cm
Silver, copper, brass, aluminum, titanium,
paper; hand fabricated, anodized, oxidized

SUSAN SKOCZEN
Knoll's Edge ▥ 2006
5.5 x 3.7 x 4 cm
Sterling silver, flocking, paint;
fabricated, oxidized
PHOTO BY DAN FOX, LUMINA STUDIO

FACING PAGE
ANDREW WELCH
*Tube-Ring Series: Dots, Infinity,
Droplet, and Holes* ▥ 2010
Largest: 6 x 5.8 x 2.5 cm
Sterling silver, enamel paint; lost
wax cast, rapid prototyped
PHOTO BY GRANT HANCOCK

DOMINIQUE LABORDERY
*Platinum Groove: A Pas de Deux
of Geometrical Shapes* ■ 2009

5 x 2 x 3 cm
Platinum
PHOTO BY PGI GERMANY

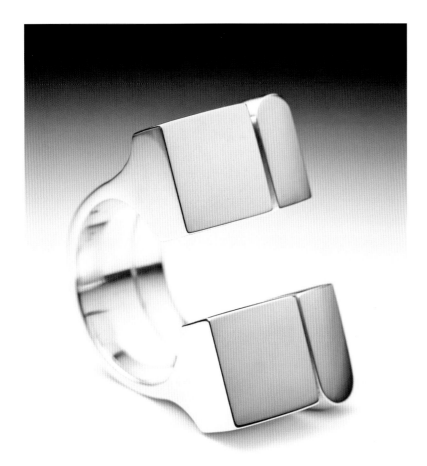

BARBARA AMZALLAG
Butterfly ■ 2006
Large ring: 2 x 2.7 x 1 cm; small ring: 2 x 2.7 x 0.5 cm
Sterling silver; hand carved, cast, hand polished

MOMOKO KUMAI
Untitled ■ 2007
0.8 x 2.2 x 2.2 cm
18-karat gold; soldered
PHOTO BY REINA SENGA

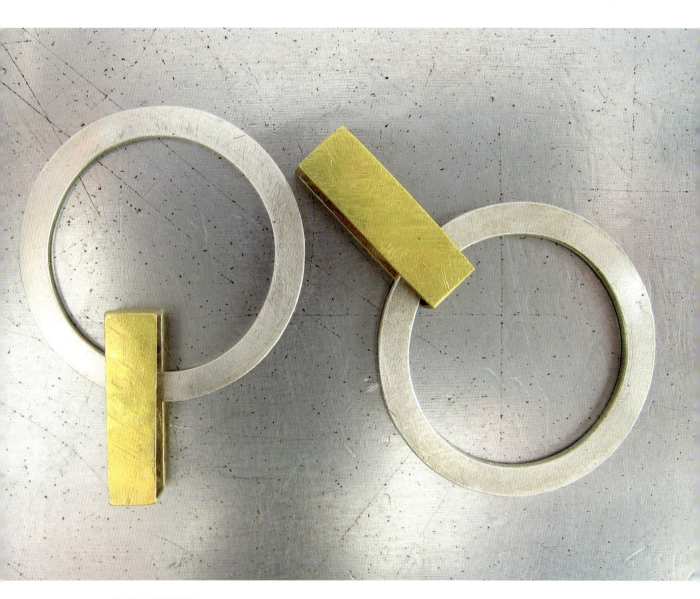

LIANA PATSURIA
Geometri ▪ 2009

Each: 3 cm in diameter
Sterling silver, 18-karat gold; hand fabricated
PHOTO BY ARTIST

ANASTASIA KANDARAKI
Untitled ■ 2010

4.5 x 4 x 2 cm
Sterling silver; oxidized
PHOTO BY FEDERICO CAVICCHIOLI

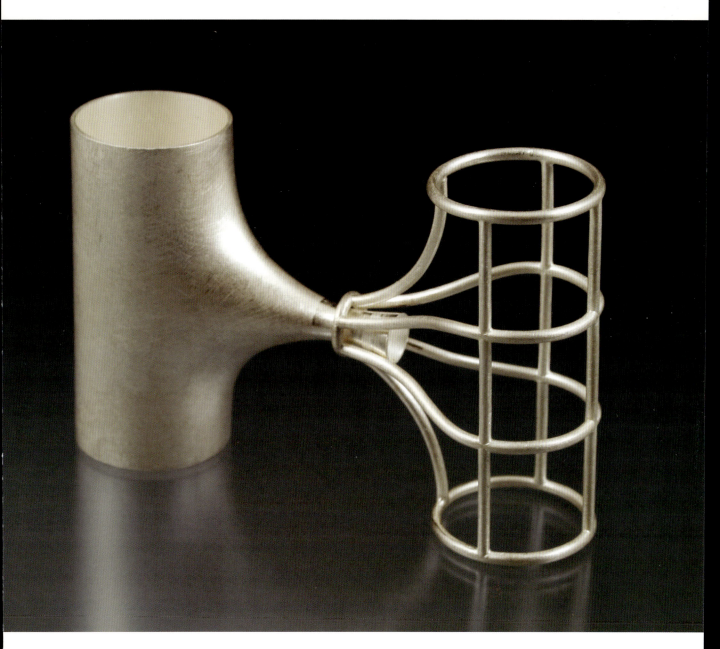

SUN KYOUNG KIM
Pair ■ 2008
5.1 x 7.6 x 2.5 cm
Sterling silver; fabricated
PHOTO BY ARTIST

YOKO TAKIRAI
Vuotoo ■ 2010
4.2 x 4.2 x 3 cm
Sterling silver, gold plate
PHOTO BY MARCO BONUCCI

KATIE POTERALA
Mokume Bling Rings ■ 2010

Worn together: 7.6 x 8.9 x 7.6 cm
Copper, nickel, brass, sterling silver;
mokume gane, fabricated, oxidized
PHOTO BY ARTIST

ERIK TIDĐNG
No Turning Back ■ 2009
Left: 2 cm in diameter; right: 1.8 cm in diameter
Sterling silver, gold plate
PHOTO BY ARTIST

KARL FRITSCH
Bum ■ 2003
6 x 4 x 5 cm
24-karat gold,
14-karat gold; oxidized
PHOTO BY ARTIST

These rings were fabricated from textiles filled with opium-scented gold dust. Their wearers will leave behind a trace of scented dust everywhere they go. The trace will evoke memories of the ring, the wearer, and the moment of contact. —SB

SOFIE BOONS
The Memory of Scents ■ 2010
Each: 3 x 3 x 2.5 cm
Essential oil, wire, fabric, gold dust; fabricated
PHOTOS BY ARTIST

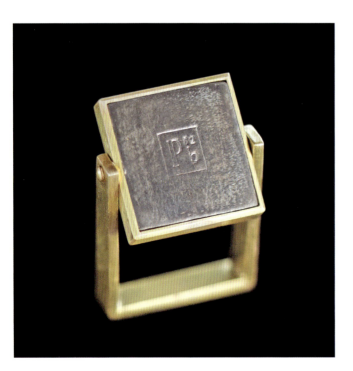

ARIEL KUPFER
Lead or Gold ■ 2004
2 x 2 x 1.7 cm
18-karat gold, lead; forged,
filed, soldered, stamped
PHOTOS BY EDUARDO TORRES

SOLVEIGA KRIVICIAI
ALFREDAS KRIVICIAI
Unengagement Ring: F--- off with Your Money,
Engagement Ring, and Marriage Contract!!! ■ 2010
3.6 x 2.9 x 3.6 cm
Sterling silver, gold engagement ring with
diamonds, ashes of a marriage contract, glass
PHOTO BY ARTIST

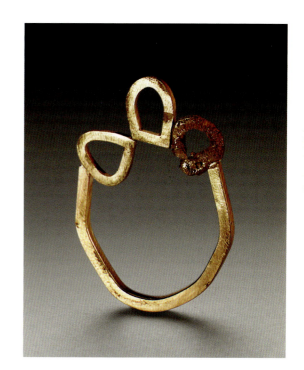

SUSAN SKOCZEN
Obvious ■ 2005
2.5 x 2.5 x 0.6 cm
18-karat gold; fabricated
PHOTO BY DAN FOX

ASHLEY BUCHANAN
Diamonds Are for Everyone ■ 2009

Ring: 3 x 2.5 x 2.5 cm
Sterling silver, magazine paper, plastic,
steel; handmade, soldered, formed
PHOTO BY JOSHUA DUDLEY GREER

NICOLE WALGER
For Good Times and Bad Times ■ 2007
5.5 x 3.5 x 0.4 cm
24-karat gold
PHOTOS BY ARTIST

YAEL FRIEDMAN
Will You Marry Me #23 ▩ 2009
5 x 3 x 0.3 cm
Brass; photo etched
PHOTO BY NIR FRIEDMAN

KATE BAUMAN
'Til Death Do Us Part ■ 2006
7.6 x 10.2 x 0.6 cm
Sterling silver, cubic zirconia; cast
PHOTOS BY ARTIST

SERIN OH
Imitation and Deception ■ 2011
6.2 x 6.1 x 6.3 cm
Sterling silver; wax cast
PHOTO BY GWANG-CHOO PARK

KARL FRITSCH
Bing ■ 2007
4 x 1.8 x 1 cm
18-karat gold, synthetic red spinel
PHOTO BY ARTIST

MICHAEL DALE BERNARD
Wood Be Diamonds Hi Def Emerald ■ 2011

4.5 x 5.5 x 3 cm
Copper, steel, hardwood,
powder coat; carved, painted
PHOTO BY ARTIST

I drew inspiration for these rings from the vibrant culture and bustling streets of India. It was my desire to capture the details of colorful saris, ancient architecture, and intricate Jali screens. I utilized the processes of hand coloring and anodizing to create vivid and unique blends of color. —MO

YURY BYLKOV
Polyring ■ 2010
6 x 6 x 6 cm
Sterling silver, cold enamel; cast
PHOTO BY ARTIST

TOP
MEGHAN O'ROURKE
Jali Rings ■ 2008
Each: 1 x 1.5 x 1.5 cm
Aluminum; hand dyed, anodized, stamped, engraved, drilled, sandblasted, embossed
PHOTO BY TOM ROSCHI

MARINA SHEETIKOFF
Confetti Cutout ◼ 2009
2.7 x 2.5 x 1 cm
Niobium; water-jet cut, anodic oxidation
PHOTO BY FERNANDO LASZLO

KELLY L. ROBINSON
Graffiti Study #1 ■ 2010

7.5 x 6.4 x 3.5 cm
Sterling silver, copper, clear plastic sheeting,
cultured pearls, paint, patina
PHOTO BY ANNIE PENNINGTON

CHUN-LUNG HSIEH
Value of Light ■ 2010

8 x 6 x 6 cm
Compact disc, brass; sawed,
soldered, hand fabricated
PHOTO BY TSANG-HSUAN LIN

DANIEL MICHEL
There Is No Single Story ■ 2010
7 x 11.9 x 9.2 cm
Plastic, paper, ink, polypropylene; rapid prototyped
(selective laser sintering), lenticular printed, CNC laser cut
PHOTOS BY ARTIST

115

SIRJA KNAAPI
Kro ■ 2011
5.5 x 5 x 0.6 cm
Aluminum, plastic, paint; riveted
PHOTO BY TOMMI PARKKINEN

GAIL MACMILLAN-LEAVITT
Untitled ■ 2011
Top: 6 x 9.5 x 4.4 cm; bottom: 6.2 x 9.5 x 2.5 cm
Lucite, resin, steel; hand cut, cold connected
PHOTOS BY DAVID PEARLMAN

NATALIA SALDIAS DONOSO
Green Wind ▪ 2010

3.5 x 3 x 1.5 cm
Sterling silver, horsehair, tissue; knitted, hand fabricated
PHOTO BY PABLO ANDRÉS VENEGAS ROMERO

MARTHA GIRALDO
Cell Phone ■ 2011

2.3 x 3.4 x 3.2 cm
Sterling silver, shibuishi, cell phone circuit
board, resin; soldered, hand fabricated
PHOTO BY ALEXI WIEDEMANN

LIAUNG CHUNG YEN
Changeability ■ 2009

Average size: 7.5 x 7.5 x 7.5 cm
Sterling silver, recycled plastic bottle caps,
recycled plastic file folder, rubber; fabricated
PHOTO BY ARTIST

NATALIE SMITH
Zero ■ 2010
7.5 x 7 x 5.5 cm
Plastic, textiles, steel, sugar
PHOTO BY ARTIST

YOUNJI CHOI
Ring ■ 2010
2.5 x 3 x 2 cm
Photopolymers; 3D printed, dyed
PHOTO BY MYUNG WOOK HUH

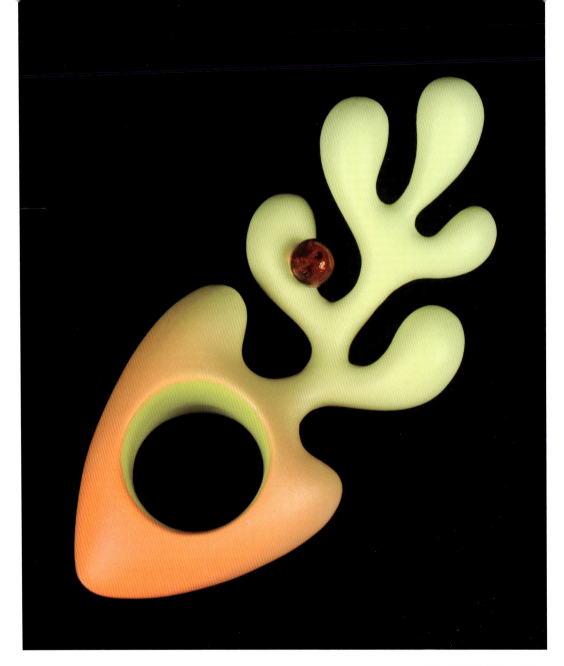

JEFFREY LLOYD DEVER
Matisse Revisited ■ 2011

8.9 x 3.8 x 0.8 cm
Polymer clay, reclaimed glass bead, steel,
cardstock; fabricated, sculpted, assembled
PHOTO BY GREGORY R. STALEY

JOHN-THOMAS RICHARD
Untitled ■ 2011
10 x 2.5 x 10 cm
Ceramic, underglaze, low-fire glaze
PHOTO BY ROBLY GLOVER

JILLIAN MOORE
Blue Double Cuppers Ring ■ 2010

5 x 3 x 1.3 cm
Polymer clay, brass, epoxy resin, paint; fabricated
PHOTO BY ARTIST

Inspired by urban pop culture, these knuckle dusters feature bezel-set, hand-painted acrylic nails. The rings symbolize the relationship that exists between femininity, gender, and violence. —IT

ISLAY TAYLOR
Pro Nailz ■ 2010
Each: 4.5 x 7.5 x 2 cm
Gold-plated bronze,
acrylic nails; hand painted
PHOTOS BY MAUREEN KEAVENY

125

JOKE DUBBELDAM
Untitled ■ 2009
2 x 1.5 x 2 cm
18-karat gold; punched, sawn, soldered
PHOTO BY ARTIST

YAEL HERMAN
22K-Gold Crushed Ring ■ 2008
2.8 x 2.8 x 1.5 cm
22-karat gold, marquise diamond; handmade, crushed
PHOTO BY NATAN DVIR

KIM ERIC LILOT
Tribute to a Genius ■ 2009

3.5 x 2.4 x 2 cm
18-karat yellow gold, Australian fire opal;
lost wax cast, chased, engraved
PHOTO BY HAP SAKWA

LEFT
DOMINIQUE LABORDERY
e_ring ■ 2008
2 x 4 x 3 cm
Silver, gold
PHOTO BY STUDIO GREEN

TOP
BARBARA HEINRICH
Wrapped Gold Ring ■ 2010
1.1 x 2.2 x 2.2 cm
18-karat yellow gold;
hand fabricated, formed
PHOTO BY TIM CALLAHAN

MARGARETH SANDSTRÖM
Untitled ■ 2011
3.6 x 3 x 5.2 cm
18-karat gold; hollow formed
PHOTO BY ARTIST

LOREE RODKIN
Bondage Ring ■ 2011
2.5 x 6 cm
18-karat white gold, black
rhodium, brown diamonds
PHOTO BY JOHNA HERNANDEZ

DMITRIY PAVLOV
Eternal Tomorrow (Wedding Ring Set) ■ 2008
Left: 1.2 x 2.4 x 2.7 cm; right: 1 x 2.1 x 2.3 cm
18-karat yellow gold, diamonds; pierced, bent, sculpted, engraved, textured

INBAL SHOMRONI
Metal Buds ■ 2010
3.5 x 1.9 x 0.1 cm
Sterling silver, 18-karat gold plate, brass
PHOTO BY ANNAT ZILBERMAN GENDLIN

NOELLE LEONE
Leone Gladiator Ring ■ 2010

2 x 2 x 2 cm
18-karat yellow gold
PHOTO BY RALPH GABRINER

135

GRAZIANO VISINTIN
Untitled ◼ 2010
Largest: 2 cm
Yellow gold, white gold, enamel
PHOTO BY MASSIMO SORMONTA

EMANUELA DUCA
Fiamma Ring ■ 2010

3.4 x 3.4 x 1 cm
Sterling silver, 23-karat gold leaf;
oxidized, wax sculpted
PHOTO BY RON BOSZKO

JANE BOWDEN
Woven Ring ■ 2008
14 x 4.6 x 4.3 cm
Sterling silver, 18-karat white gold; hand woven
PHOTO BY GRANT HANCOCK

BARBARA COHEN
Ties That Bind ■ 2010
7 x 2.5 x 1.8 cm
Iron, pyrite, latex; fabricated, wrapped
PHOTO BY ARTIST

TAISHI HAMADA
No Form ■ 2006
2.9 x 2.2 x 1 cm
Glass; laser sculpted
PHOTO BY TAKAYUKI SERI

GEOFF RIGGLE
Form Study Five #2: Plato's Release ■ 2009
15 x 2 x 5 cm
Sterling silver, polyurethane; fabricated, cast
PHOTO BY JEFF SABO

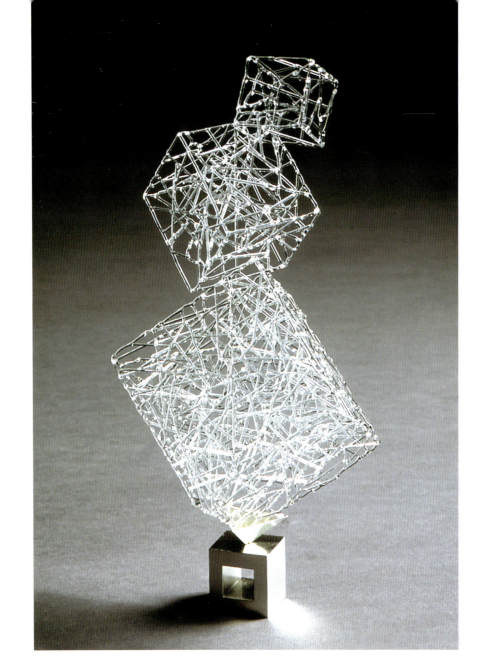

EUNSUH CHOI
Progression II ■ 2007
25 x 20 x 20 cm
Sterling silver, glass; flameworked
PHOTO BY ARTHUR CHEN

GITTA PIELCKE
Salt-Ring ■ 2009
4.3 x 2.8 x 2.5 cm
Sterling silver, salt crystal
PHOTO BY ARTIST

RUUDT PETERS
Sefiroth Abba ■ 2011
12.5 x 5.5 x 9 cm
Silver, glass; oxidized
PHOTO BY ARTIST

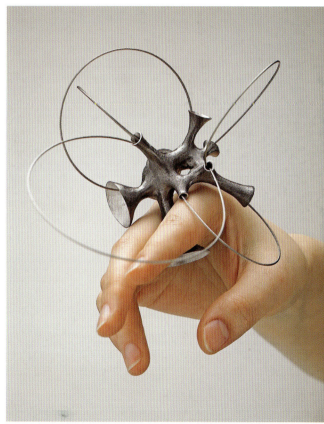

CHAE SEKANG
Contacts ■ 2009

Each: 6 x 7 x 5 cm
Copper, stainless steel, sterling silver;
electroformed, fabricated, plated
PHOTOS BY MYUNG WOOK HUH

MARK EDGOOSE
Ring and Box No. 4 ■ 2010
3.8 x 2.7 x 2.7 cm
Niobium, titanium
PHOTO BY JEREMY DILLON

SATOSHI NAKAMURA
Boxes Rings 01 ■ 2010
Each: 2.8 x 2.8 x 1.4 cm
Sterling silver; CAD, fused
deposition modeled, lost wax cast
PHOTO BY PETRA JASCHKE

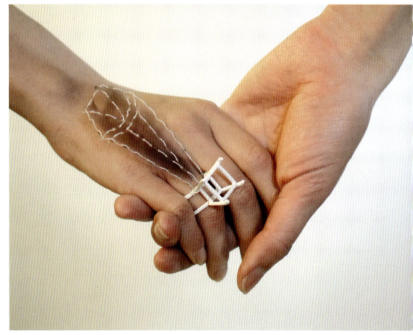

I-HSUAN KUO
Fantasy ▪ 2011
10 x 2 x 4 cm
Copper, lacquer, transparency
PHOTOS BY ARTIST

YOUNSEAL EUM
Forever and Ever ■ 2009
13 x 8 x 8 cm
Sterling silver; soldered, cast
PHOTO BY ARTIST

149

SUNG YEOUL LEE

Connection ▨ 2007

Each: 2.5 x 5.1 x 8.6 cm
Sterling silver, resin,
jute rope; cast, fabricated
PHOTO BY ARTIST

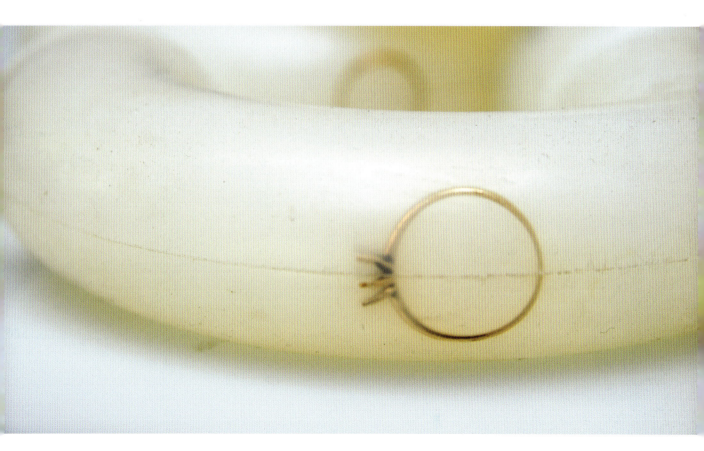

MAYA KINI
Aether ■ 2007
12.5 x 10.5 x 4 cm
Silicone, found and fabricated
gold rings, sink traps; cast
PHOTO BY ARTIST

This set of rings questions how today's society defines a community and how our systems of value have the potential to change as natural resources grow scarce. The rings place common drinking water in a position of high importance, examining the value it might hold in the future, even to the wealthiest of societies. —EK

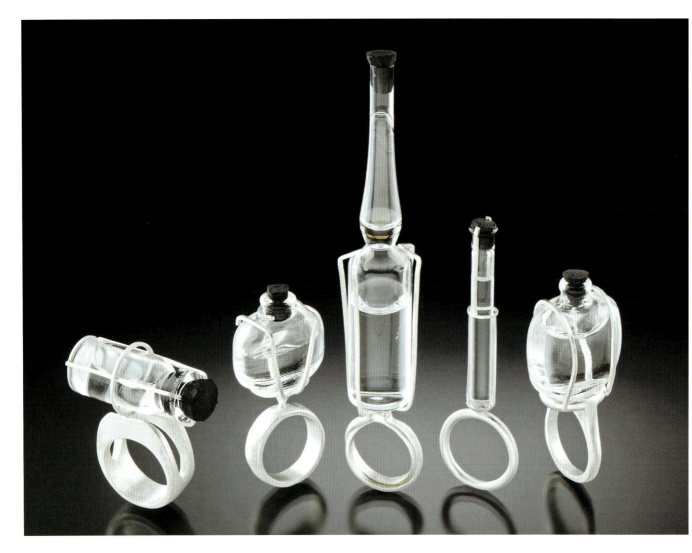

EMILY KLOPSTEIN
Precious Material ■ 2010

Tallest: 11.4 x 2 x 2 cm
Sterling silver, found objects,
rubber, water; cast, fabricated
PHOTO BY LARRY SANDERS

An engagement ring is a symbol of love, a visual statement of the bond between two people. *Engagement Ring—Understanding a Connection* is both an audible and visible representation of this bond. The plastic "diamond" houses a small microphone. When placed over a partner's heart, the microphone picks up the sound of the beat, which is then projected through copper brooches that house two small speakers. Without a partner, the piece will not function—much like a marriage. **—CB**

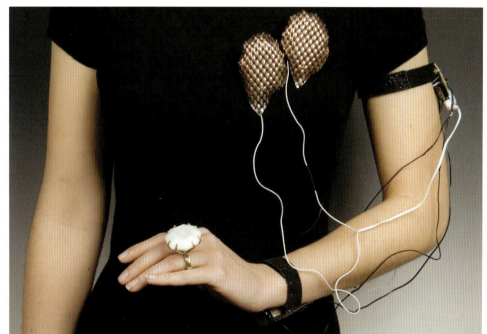

CHRISTIANA BYRNE
Engagement Ring—Understanding a Connection ■ 2009
Ring: 4.8 x 3.8 x 3.8 cm; brooch: 7.6 x 5 x 2.5 cm
Copper, brass, plastic, microphone, speakers, electrical wiring, battery,
hook-and-loop tape, circuit board; cast, hydraulic pressed, oxidized
PHOTOS BY ERICA VOSS

153

FACING PAGE
CRISTINA ROQUE
Dedication Ring ■ 2011

Written ring: 3 x 3 x 1.3 cm;
unwritten ring: 2.8 x 2.8 x 1.4 cm
Paper pulp, glue; molded
PHOTO BY TIAGO REIS

SHIRI AVDA
Biology of a Dream ■ 2010

8.5 x 4.8 x 1.5 cm
Sterling silver, 24-karat gold,
book paper, ink; hand fabricated
PHOTO BY TAL SCHIFFMAN

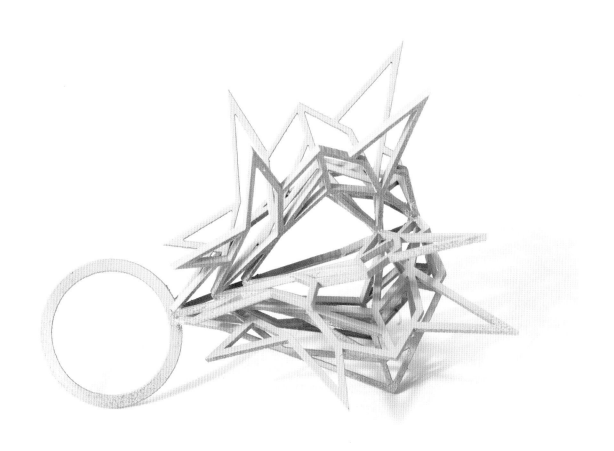

MYIA BONNER
Rough Diamond Ring ▨ 2010

5 x 5 cm
Clear plastic sheeting; laser cut,
dyed, hand assembled
PHOTO BY ARTIST

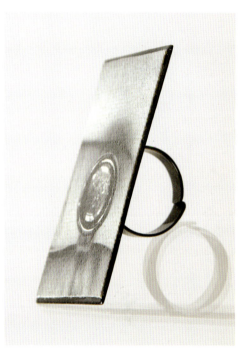

ADRIANA LISOWSKA
ANETA LIS-MARCINKIEWICZ
Imitation ■ 2006
2 x 6 x 3.5 cm
Copper, photograph, canvas, acrylic;
soldered, cut, printed, covered
PHOTOS BY MARTA SULKOWSKA

CINDY J. COOK

Bzzz ■ 2010

18 x 2.5 x 1.5 cm

Sterling silver, bumblebee; hand fabricated

PHOTO BY ARTIST 10051

KERIANNE QUICK
Untitled ■ 2009
14 x 3 x 0.5 cm
Sterling silver, granulated sugar; fabricated
PHOTO BY ARTIST

MI-MI MOSCOW
From the Frog Can Fly Series: Ring of Prometheus ■ 2005
3.5 x 17 x 1.5 cm
Frog, melhior, acrylic, coloring
PHOTO BY ARTISTS

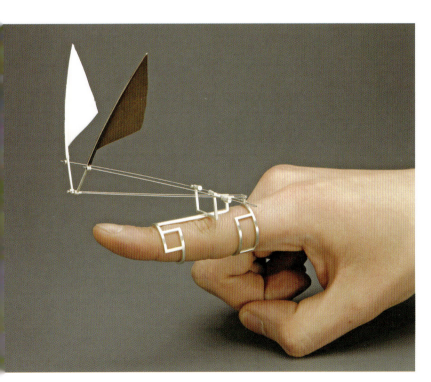
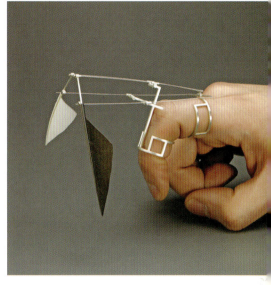

DUKNO YOON
Suspended Wings ■ 2003

6 x 8 x 8 cm
Sterling silver, stainless steel, feathers
PHOTOS BY MYUNG-WOOK HUH

161

ALEXANDER FRIEDRICH
Steamulator ▨ 2010

5 x 3 x 1 cm
Copper; sawed, soldered, bent
PHOTO BY ARTIST

AMANDA PACKER
Untitled ■ 2008

11.5 x 4.5 x 3.5 cm
Copper, enamel
PHOTO BY DIANNE REILLY

163

JOHANNA DAHM
Clay ■ 2008
4 x 3 x 1.4 cm
22-karat gold, steel wire
PHOTO BY REINHARD ZIMMERMANN

JED GREEN
Untitled ■ 2011

5.5 x 5.5 x 6 cm
Glass, paint, ceramic transfer, silver,
freshwater pearls; lamp blown, hand painted
PHOTOS BY RUSSELL SADUR

SAMANTHA R. GRAY
Amber Ring Pop ■ 2008
6 x 3.5 x 3.5 cm
Sterling silver, nickel, amber; hollow constructed
PHOTO BY TOM BLAKELY

SUMIKO HATTORI
Untitled ■ 2004
Each: 3.4 x 4.9 x 4.4 cm
Silver, stone
PHOTO BY HITOSHI NISHIYAMA

VICTOR SALDARRIAGA
Vaina Abierta ■ 2010
2.9 x 3.2 cm
Silver, patina, 24-karat gold plate, wax; oxidized
PHOTO BY ANDRÉS GÓMEZ

ROBERT THOMAS MULLEN
Exquisite Security ■ 2010

5.1 x 8.3 x 3.2 cm
Sterling silver, 22-karat gold,
patina; lost wax cast, oxidized
PHOTO BY ARTIST

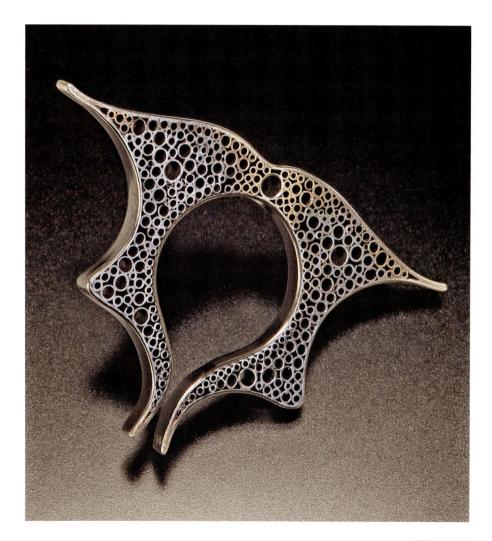

VINA RUST
Ring #1: Stained Cell Series ■ 2005

5.5 x 3.5 x 0.3 cm
Sterling silver, 14-karat gold, liver
of sulfur patina; hand fabricated
PHOTO BY DOUG YAPLE

LUCIA BEHMER
Watchtower Ring on Chain ■ 2011
Ring: 5.7 x 2.7 x 1.8 cm
Sterling silver, brass, quartz; pierced,
soldered, cold connected, oxidized
PHOTOS BY MARK BREHMER

SUN LI
Part I ■ 2009
Each: 2.2 x 2.2 x 1 cm
Sterling silver, rhodium plate
PHOTO BY STUDIO MUNCH

BEN NEUBAUER
Dome Ring ■ 2004
4.5 x 4.5 x 4.5 cm
Sterling silver, 18-karat gold;
fabricated, oxidized
PHOTO BY COURTNEY FRISSE

GIOVANNI SICURO 'MINTO'
Untitled ■ 2010

4.6 x 4 x 2.7 cm
Silver, niello, 24-karat gold;
hollow constructed, gilded
PHOTO BY ARTIST

GREGORY LARIN
Gory Story ■ 2010
Largest: 15 x 2.5 cm
Silver, plastic
PHOTO BY ALEX KUCHERENKO

FACING PAGE
RACHEL TIMMINS
Growth One ■ 2010
60 x 60 x 60 cm
Foam, craft glitter, epoxy resin; carved
PHOTO BY JOSEPH HYDE

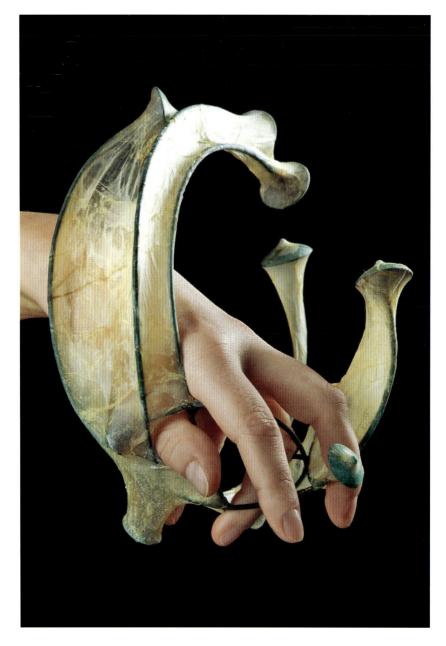

HOLLAND HOUDEK
From the Cognizance Series: Bound ▪ 2010
17.8 x 20.3 x 14 cm
Copper, liver of sulfur, pig gut; hand fabricated
PHOTO BY ARTIST

KERI STRAKA
Coiled ■ 2011
Large ring: 5 x 5.8 x 1 cm
Porcelain clay, copper oxide stain, red enamel paint,
sculptural background form; fired in oxidation, cone 6
PHOTO BY ARTIST

SIGAL MESHORER
Lost Stones ■ 2010

Each: 3.1 x 3 x 1.5 cm
Clay, glass, brass; hand fabricated,
electric fired, cone 5
PHOTO BY AVRAHAM HAY

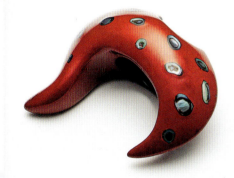

YUN SANGHEE
Red Ring (A Ring That Cannot Clench My Fist) ■ 2006

3 x 6.5 x 5.7 cm
Asian lacquer, wood, mother-of-pearl
PHOTOS BY STUDIO MUNCH

181

MEL MILLER
Mnemochronology, No. 3
(Object with Removable Rings) ■ 2009

19 x 8 x 7 cm
Fine silver, enamel, fabric,
felted wool; fused, repoussé, sewn
PHOTO BY JEREMY DILLON

KERIANNE QUICK
Untitled ■ 2009
4.5 x 4.5 x 3.5 cm
Sterling silver, granulated sugar; fabricated
PHOTO BY ARTIST

MONICA CECCHI
Left: *Mondo;* right: *Nidi* ▬ 2010

Largest: 6 x 4 x 4 cm
Tin cans; cut, cold-
temperature assembly
PHOTOS BY GIUSTINO CHEMELLO

The cups around the edge of *Wind Wheel* capture the breath of the wearer, which sets the ring in motion. As it rotates, the ring produces a lonesome, squeaking sound reminiscent of an empty swing set. The ring moves with the wearer and is moved by the wearer. —CM

CLAIRE MCARDLE
Wind Wheel ■ 2010
14 x 12 x 4 cm
Sterling silver; formed, soldered
PHOTO BY JEREMY DILLON

LITAL MENDEL
Folds ■ 2009
Largest: 6 x 6 x 4 cm
Paper, aluminum, screws,
lacquer; origami, laser cut
PHOTO BY NOA KEDMI

187

GRAZIANO VISINTIN
Untitled ■ 2006

Largest: 1.7 x 1.5 cm
Yellow gold, white gold, enamel
PHOTO BY MASSIMO SORMONTA

GIOVANNI CORVAJA
Colorful Enamel Ring ■ 2007
1.9 x 1.6 x 1 cm
18-karat gold, glass enamel;
hand-drawn wire, constructed
PHOTO BY ARTIST

CYNTHIA EID
Golden Digit Wave ■ 2010
3 x 2.5 x 1 cm
Argentium sterling silver, 22-karat yellow gold;
synclastic raising, anticlastic raising
PHOTO BY ARTIST

ANNEKE SCHAT
The Unexpected Delusion ▪ 2008

6.1 x 7.4 x 3.2 cm
Sterling silver, 18-karat gold, rock crystal, tourmaline
PHOTO BY JAN WILLEM DE JONG

JORGE GIL
Kama Sutra ■ 2011

2.7 x 2.1 x 2.4 cm
Titanium, 18-karat gold; forged,
electrolysis colored, sanded
PHOTO BY RAUL CASAS ANCA

SADIE WANG
Gold Leaf Flower Ring with Pearl ■ 2011

2.8 x 2.8 x 5.1 cm
18-karat gold and silver bimetal, sterling
silver, pearl; hand fabricated
PHOTO BY JOHN LUCAS

193

GAYLE EASTMAN
Aqua Pool ◼ 2009

2.5 x 1.9 x 3.2 cm
18-karat gold, 22-karat gold,
aquamarine; forged
PHOTO BY RALPH GABRINER

JEE HYE KWON
Primavera ■ 2010

7.5 x 9.5 x 6 cm
Sterling silver, topaz;
oxidized, hand fabricated
PHOTO BY RALPH GABRINER

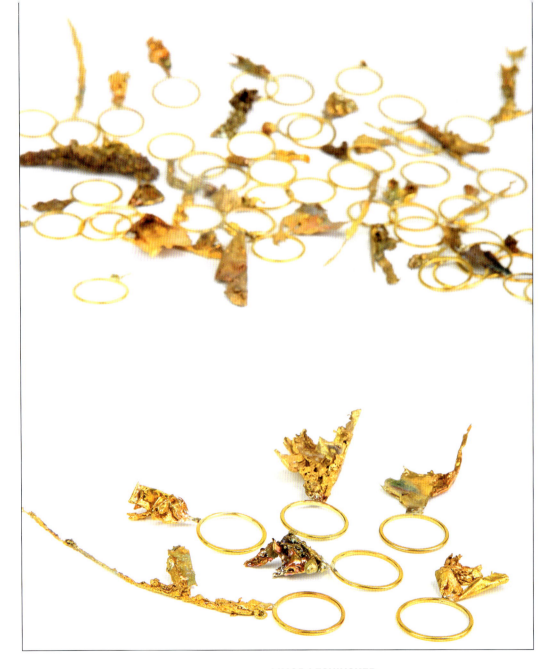

LIMOR LESHINSKER
Untitled ■ 2010

Largest: 9 x 3.7 x 1 cm
Brass, casting waste
PHOTO BY RAANAN COHEN

PATRIZIA BONATI
Ring for Two ■ 2010
4 x 6.5 x 1 cm
18-karat gold plate,
white enamel; chiseled
PHOTO BY ARTIST

JOHANNA DAHM
Clay ■ 2008
4.5 x 5.4 x 3.3 cm
18-karat gold, pure silver, diamond dust,
steel, rough black diamonds
PHOTO BY RIENHARD ZIMMERMANN

KIRA SEIDEN
Magic Garden ■ 2010
3.5 x 1.5 cm
Resin
PHOTO BY ARTIST

Through the abstract construction of these rings, I avoid suggesting how they should be worn. Instead, the construction encourages play and experimentation by the wearers. —FAD

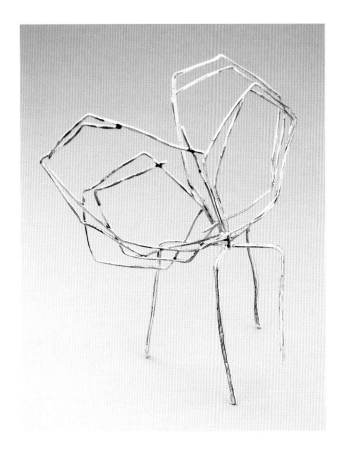

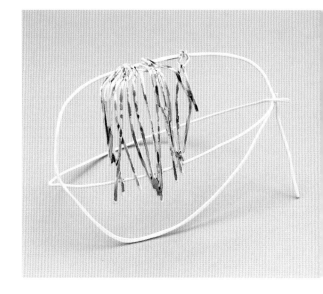

FARRAH AL-DUJAILI
Untitled ▓ 2010
Left: 7 x 10 x 11.5 cm; right: 7.5 x 6 x 5 cm
Copper, enamel paint, pencil, watercolor; soldered, laser welded
PHOTOS BY ARTIST

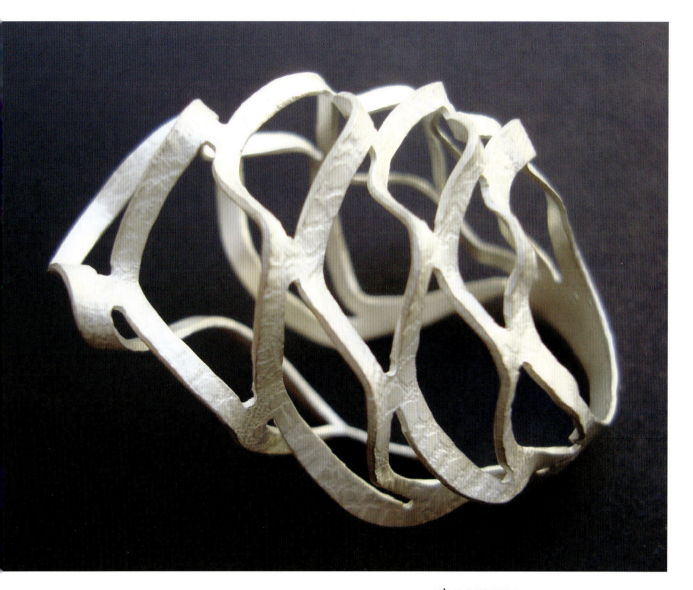

NÈLE CONTENT
Untitled ■ 2009
5 x 3.5 x 2.5 cm
Sterling silver, laminated print; folded
PHOTO BY ARTIST

LAURA MAINS
Untitled ■ 2011
5 x 7 x 2 cm
Silver, white finish;
pierced, scored, folded
PHOTO BY ARTIST

I enjoy juxtaposing organic, life-based materials with industrial metals. In the case of *December's End*, the juxtaposition lies in the partnering of caribou antler with sterling silver. While both materials come from the earth, they're very different to work with and provide different tactile and visual qualities. **—AK**

ADRIENNE KRIEGER
December's End ■ 2011
2.2 x 2.2 x 0.9 cm
Caribou antler, sterling silver;
carved, CAD, engraved
PHOTO BY ARTIST

203

GULAR MUSTAFA
Someday I'll Return ■ 2011
5 x 3.5 x 3 cm
Silver, polymer clay, gold, paper, ink, wax
PHOTO BY BRAM LAMERS

GAL KUPERMAN
Untitled ▪ 2008

5 x 3.3 x 3.2 cm
Brass, paint; constructed
PHOTO BY ARTIST

TOP
ANNA LINDSAY MACDONALD
Queensway Ring Set ▪ 2006

Each: 2 x 4 x 2 cm
Sterling silver, laminated paper;
hand pierced, hand cut
PHOTO BY STEVE LEE

EMANUELA DUCA
Sand Ring ■ 2009
2.8 x 4.4 x 1.4 cm
Sterling silver, diamonds;
oxidized, wax sculpted
PHOTO BY RON BOSZKO

KATIE GRUBER
20 Centimeters of Snow ■ 2009
7 x 7.5 x 6.5 cm
Copper, sterling silver,
acrylic paint, tile paint; forged
PHOTO BY FEDERICO CAVICCHIOLI

MARINA ANTONIOU
Stalk | *2009*
2 x 4 x 2 cm
Sterling silver;
hand forged, soldered
PHOTO BY ARTIST

STEFANIA LUCCHETTA
Digital 65 Ring ■ 2008
3 x 4.5 x 4 cm
Stellite, 18-karat white gold, diamond;
rapid prototyped, hand polished
PHOTO BY ARTIST

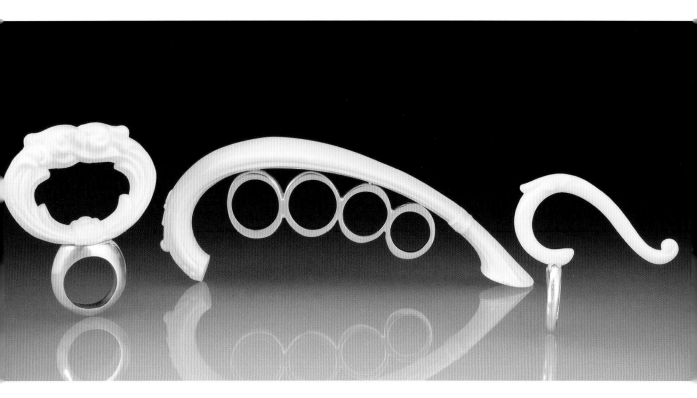

EMILY SECOY
Hold Series ▧ 2011

Various dimensions
Plastic, sterling silver; cast, fabricated
PHOTO BY ABBY JOHNSTON

LI-CHU WU
Untitled ■ 2010
6.5 x 5 x 5 cm
Paper; laser cut

ANJA EICHLER
Untitled ■ 2011

4 x 4 x 7 cm
Work glove, sterling silver;
hand fabricated, painted
PHOTO BY FEDERIC CAVICCHIOLI

211

BRIDGET CATCHPOLE
Tangle Rings ■ 2008

Each: 4.4 x 2.5 x 3.4 cm
Sterling silver, upcycled plastic
PHOTO BY ANTHONY MCLEAN

FELIEKE VAN DER LEEST
Prima Ballerina Hippo-Lolita ■ 2008
6 x 6 x 7.5 cm
Plastic animal, textile, bone, gold,
cubic zirconia; crocheted, metalsmithing
PHOTOS BY EDDO HARTMANN

ADVA ROZENSHTEIN
Fun Rings ▪ 2009
Each: 4 x 2 x 0.6 cm
Sterling silver, rubber balloons,
zircon, plastic; wrapped
PHOTO BY ROY MIZRACHI

JULIA BORZENKO
The Island of the Rainbow Elephants ■ 2010

Various dimensions
Sterling silver, polymer clay; wax modeled, cast, soldered
PHOTO BY YURY BYLKOV

215

AURELIO CASTAÑO
Garden Pond Ring ■ 2010
4 x 3.5 x 3.5 cm
Seed beads, rivoli beads, discarded plastic monofilament;
peyote stitch, herringbone stitch, netting
PHOTO BY ARTIST

MARJORIE SIMON
Ring Candy: Clover/Tangerine ■ 2009

3 x 0.8 cm
Sterling silver and 22-karat gold bimetal, enamel,
copper; torch fired, embossed, oxidized
PHOTO BY KEN YANOVIAK

This ring is part of a series I designed related to scientific experiments performed on mice. The lily pads allow the mouse to breathe underwater by delivering oxygen to its brain. —EC

EMILY COBB
Lily Pad Mouse, Experiment #2 ■ 2010
10 x 7.5 x 6 cm
Polyamide, fabric dye
PHOTO BY REBECCA WADE AND ARTIST

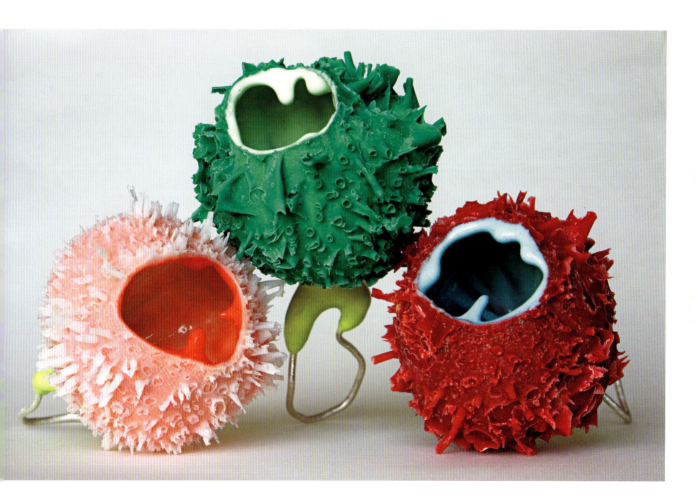

MALENE KASTALJE
And There Were Only Tiny Sounds . . . ■ 2011
Each: 8 x 4.5 x 4.5 cm
Silicone rubber, cotton, pigment, silver; cast
PHOTO BY ARTIST

URANIT BAR-NES
Links Ring ■ 2007
4 x 4.4 x 4.4 cm
Sterling silver, patina, blue
polyurethane, white and blue zircons
PHOTO BY HAGGAI YEDIDYA

FELIEKE VAN DER LEEST
Candy Rabbit Rings ■ 2010
Each: 6 x 3.5 x 3.5 cm
Textile; crocheted
PHOTO BY EDDO HARTMANN

NATALIE SMITH
Coral D ■ 2010
10.5 x 7 x 7.3 cm
Plastic, textiles, steel, sugar
PHOTO BY ARTIST

HANNAH TOMOKO JORIS
Untitled ■ 2005
4 x 2.5 x 2.6 cm
Sterling silver, porcelain; assembled
PHOTOS BY ARTIST

DHA-MEE HAHN
Lime Cluster Ring ■ 2010
10 x 10 x 10 cm
Sterling silver, artificial limes; prong set
PHOTO BY ARTIST

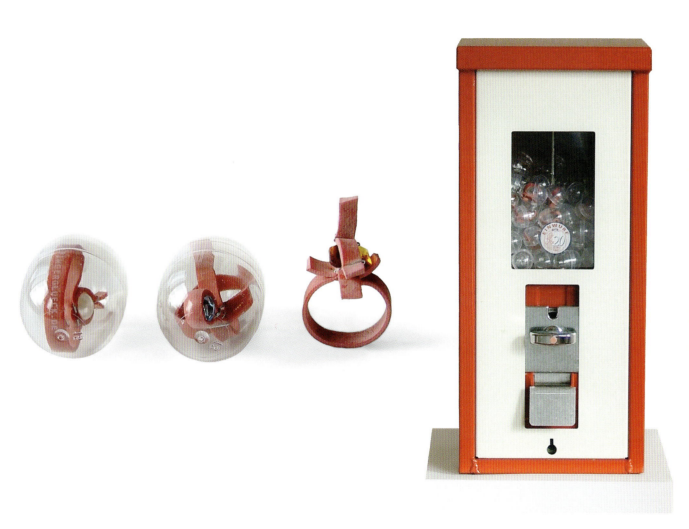

IRIS MERKLE
Untitled ■ 2004

Machine: 50 x 22.5 x 19 cm;
Each egg: 3.5 x 2.5 x 2.5 cm
Glass, plastic, rubber band
PHOTOS BY ARTIST

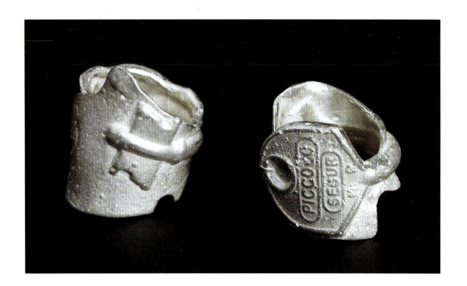

FRANCINE OEYEN
Cohabitation Rings ▪ 2010
Each: 3 x 3 x 6 cm
Sterling silver; plaster cast, lost wax process
PHOTOS BY PATRICIO CAMPINI

ANNAMARIA ZANELLA
Wheels ■ 2006
4 x 3 x 3.5 cm
Silver, enamel, gold
PHOTO BY RENZO PASQUALE

CLARE THOMPSON
Deadly Indulgence II ▦ 2011

Largest: 6.5 x 3.5 x 3.5 cm
Casting resin, epoxy resin, white chocolate, gold
leaf, silver leaf, sugar, water; molded, cast
PHOTOS BY ARTIST

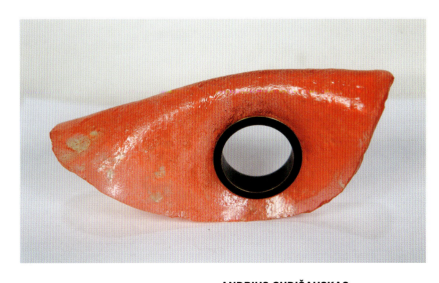

PHOTO BY CYNTHIA LEE

TOP
JESSICA J. LEE
Keepsake Rings ■ 2010
Each: 4.8 x 4.6 x 4.6 cm
Plastic bags, sterling silver; sewn, folded

ANDRIUS GUDIŠAUSKAS
Untitled ■ 2011
10.3 x 4.6 cm
Brass, nutritional gelatin

PHOTO BY ROMUALDAS EITBEVICIUS

JUDIT SANTAK
My Tooth Print for My Lover ▨ 2001
2.7 x 2.8 x 0.5 cm
Sterling silver; cast
PHOTO BY ORAVECZ ISTVÀN

JOSÉ CARLOS MARQUES
Auschwitz ■ 2011
3.5 x 4 x 3.2 cm
Human teeth, resin; assembled
PHOTO BY ARTIST

ISABEL DAMMERMANN
Run Baby Run! ■ 2010

5 x 8 x 2.5 cm
Silver, shell, polymer clay, tape;
modeled, glued, hand fabricated
PHOTO BY FEDERICO CAVICCHIOLI

EDGAR LÓPEZ JIMÉNEZ
Shell Ring ■ 2011
15 x 10 x 10 cm
Ceramic; hand shaped
PHOTO BY ARTIST

RITA MARCANGELO
Magma ■ 2011
5 x 3.5 x 3.5 cm
Silver, silk, acrylic paint; oxidized, burned
PHOTO BY ADREAN BLOOMARD

RIA LINS
Ring ■ 2009
4 x 3 x 0.7 cm
Wool, textile, embroidery thread, paint, quartz
PHOTO BY DRIES VAN DEN BRANDE

FACING PAGE▶

SHARONA MUIR
Sun Ring ■ 2010
6 x 5 x 5 cm
Mixed media, polychrome
PHOTO BY TIM THAYE

AI MORITA
Puzzle Ring ▪ 2005
5 x 3 x 3 cm
Sterling silver, resin, acrylic;
fabricated, CAD, cast, dyed
PHOTO BY ARTIST

MAUREEN BRUSA ZAPPELLINI
Country Gal Wedding ■ 2010

5 x 10 x 3.5 cm
Wooden clothespin, seed pods,
pewter, paint; assembled, fabricated
PHOTO BY ARTIST

ALIDRA ALIÐ
Orchid ◼ 2008
10 x 9 cm
Sterling silver, plastic
PHOTOS BY DORTE KROGH

BARBARA COHEN
Beginnings ■ 2011
20.5 x 3 x 1.5 cm
Sterling silver, cornhusk, 14-karat
gold, cubic zirconia; fabricated
PHOTO BY ARTIST

DHA-MEE HAHN
Fabric Flower Rings ■ 2010
Each: 7.6 x 15.2 x 15.2 cm
Sterling silver, vintage fabric; cold connected
PHOTO BY ARTIST

PETER DECKERS
SARAH READ
The Prince Is Dead; Long Live the Prince ■ 2011

Andy Warhol's Signature Ring: 3.5 x 3.3 x 2.2 cm
Campbell's Soup Can Cuff: 10 x 7 x 7 cm
Sterling silver, rubber, U.S. quarter, red inkpad, acrylic tag,
organza, thread; printed, stretched, fabricated
PHOTO BY ARTIST

JOANA RIBEIRO
Ruber Folium ▪ 2011
4.8 x 3.5 x 2.5 cm
Silver, red metallic ink; microfused
PHOTO BY MOMENTO CATIVO

Using handmade paper allowed me to layer in materials as I created this ring. The surface is enriched by those materials—graphite, thread, matchsticks—and by how those materials reacted during the papermaking process. Some layers are uncovered while others remain hidden. —MW

MELISSA WALTER
Carved Abaca Ring ■ 2010
5.1 x 3.8 x 1.3 cm
Handmade abaca paper, resin, sterling silver
PHOTO BY ARTIST

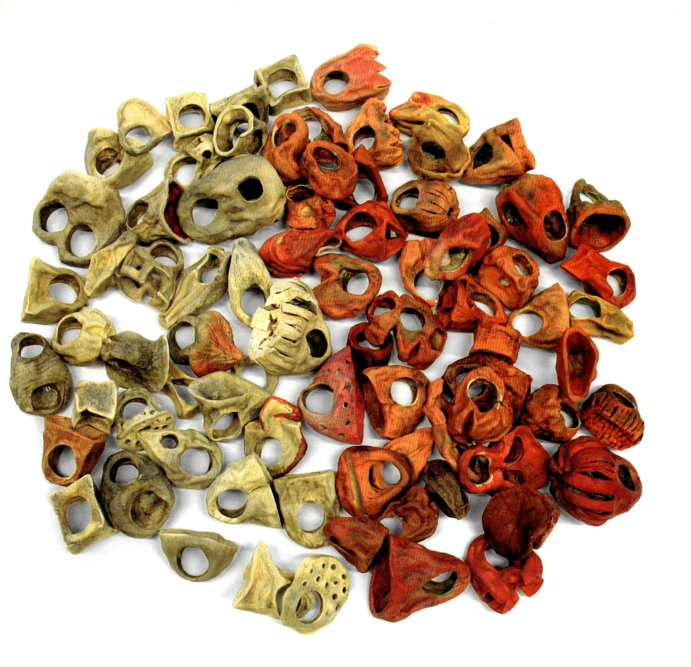

JULIE USEL
Potato Rings ■ 2006

Various dimensions
Potato; carved, dried, colored
PHOTO BY ARTIST

PATRIZIA BONATI
Ring for One ■ 2010
3.5 x 2 x 4.5 cm
18-karat yellow gold
PHOTO BY ARTIST

FACING PAGE
JANE BOWDEN
Woven Ring Series ■ 2008
Bottom ring: 11 x 4.5 x 3.7 cm
Sterling silver, 18-karat white, pink
and yellow gold; hand woven
PHOTO BY GRANT HANCOCK

SIAN ELIZABETH HUGHES
Flourish Ring ■ 2008

3 x 3 x 1 cm
Sterling silver; constructed
PHOTO BY J. HYTCH

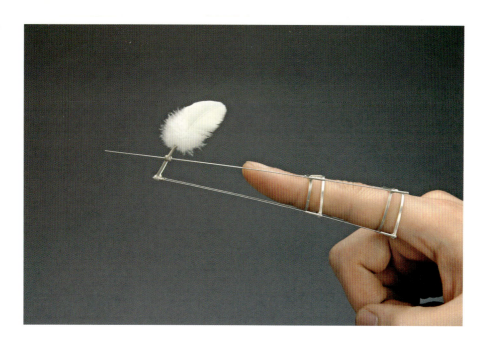

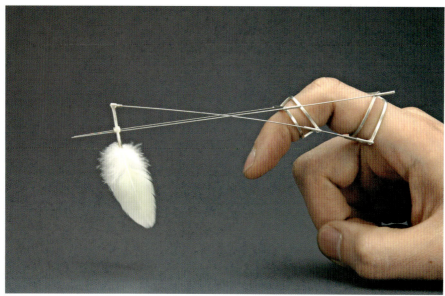

DUKNO YOON
Suspended Wings ■ 2002

4 x 9 x 12 cm
Sterling silver, stainless steel, feathers
PHOTOS BY MYUNG-WOOK HUH

ALJA NEUNER
Möglichkeiten Einer Freundschaft ■ 2011

Largest: 6 x 10 x 2 cm
18-karat gold, sterling silver, wood,
sapphire; cast, assembled, hammered
PHOTO BY CHLOË POTTER

SUN KYOUNG KIM
Between Two ■ 2008
7.6 x 7.6 x 7.6 cm
Sterling silver; fabricated
PHOTOS BY ARTIST

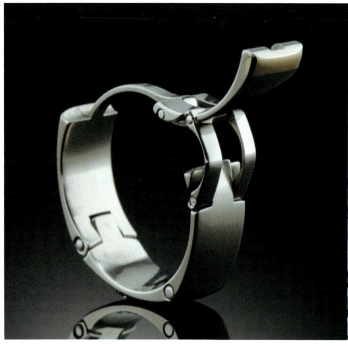

JEFF MCWHINNEY
Untitled ■ 2010
2.2 x 2.2 x 0.8 cm
Titanium, 18-karat gold; CNC machined
PHOTOS BY KIM LARSON

GEOFF RIGGLE
Form Study Five #4: Plato's Obsession ▨ 2009
7.5 x 2 x 7.5 cm
Sterling silver, polyurethane; fabricated, cast
PHOTO BY JEFF SABO

SUNG YEOUL LEE
Extended View ■ 2006
12.7 x 17.8 x 1.3 cm
Sterling silver, lenses; fabricated
PHOTO BY ARTIST

YUNG-HUEI CHAO
Window Series I ■ 2009

Each: 2 x 2 x 2 cm
Silver, nickel silver; etched, fabricated
PHOTO BY ARTIST

DANAE NATSIS
Open Cut ■ 2009

Largest: 3 x 4.3 x 4.3 cm
Sterling silver, cognac diamonds, rough
diamonds, wax; hand carved, lathe
turned, cast, set, textured, oxidized
PHOTO BY ARTIST

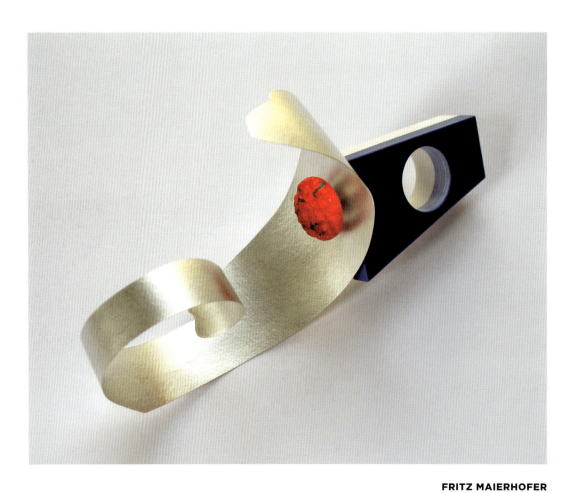

FRITZ MAIERHOFER
Studio—Ring 3 ■ 2011
11 x 7 x 4 cm
Corian, sterling silver, glass, acrylic
PHOTO BY ARTIST

FELICITY PETERS
Lest We Forget—Krakow ■ 2009

12.2 x 11.2 x 9.2 cm
Sterling silver, 24-karat gold, 18-karat
gold, paint; cast, constructed
PHOTO BY VICTOR FRANCE

SUSAN MAY
Two Rings ■ 2009

Largest: 3 x 2 cm
Sterling silver, 18-karat gold;
pierced, forged, soldered
PHOTO BY JOËL DEGEN

ANETTE RACK
Untitled ■ 2011

3 x 2 x 1 cm
Freshwater pearl, plastic; knotted
PHOTOS BY GÜNTHER DÄCHERT

SARAH NARUM
Thumb War ■ 2010

Cowboy Hat: 7.9 x 2.4 x 2.4 cm
Top Hat: 8.2 x 2.7 x 2.7 cm
Copper, patina, suede; hand
fabricated, hand sewn

BRITTNEY PHILLIP
Material Bond Ring and Bracelet ■ 20

17 x 10 x 14 cr
Copper, straw; soaked, braided
woven, wound, formed, drie

SUNG YEOUL LEE
Knot So Precious ■ 2006

Average: 3 x 8 x 2 cm
Poly rope, tool dip, aluminum; fabricated
PHOTO BY ARTIST

ANTJE STOLZ
Drink Me! ■ 2010

Each: 4 x 2.3 x 1.1 cm
Sterling silver, reconstructed red coral,
solid acrylic; sawed, cast, soldered, riveted
PHOTOS BY ARTIST

SIRJA KNAAPI
Po ■ 2011
5.7 x 5 x 0.7 cm
Aluminum, plastic, paint; riveted
PHOTO BY TOMMI PARKKINEN

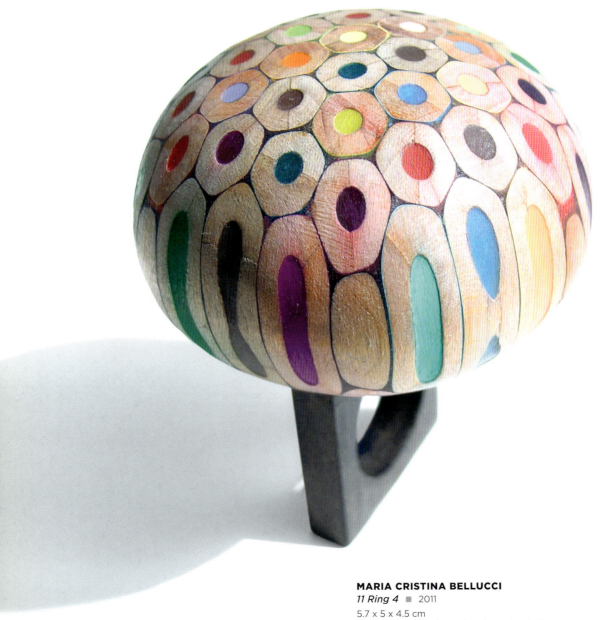

MARIA CRISTINA BELLUCCI
11 Ring 4 ■ 2011
5.7 x 5 x 4.5 cm
Colored pencils, ebony; hand constructed
PHOTO BY ARTIST

TOP
ELIN FLOGNMAN
Fat Princess ■ 2009

6.5 x 3.5 x 2.5 cm
Teak, sponge, thread, paint
PHOTO BY ARTIST

BOTTOM
GABRIELA MIGUEL
Transparencias ■ 2010

6 x 7.5 x 5.5 cm
Sterling silver, polystyrene
net; hand fabricated
PHOTO BY ALEJANDRO CRISTOFOL

This ring comes to life on the body as a three-dimensional form and then collapses once it's removed. The action of pulling the ring across the finger is what brings it to life — it's not a conscious choice by the wearer, but a moment of surprise. **—JH**

JOANNA HEMSLEY
Inter(action) ■ 2009
2 x 2 x 2 cm
Silver, 14-karat gold plating, silk; hand dyed
PHOTOS BY ARTIST

GRACE HILLIARD-KOSHINSKY
Untitled ■ 2011
8 x 5 x 2.5 cm
Sterling silver, aluminum, paper
PHOTO BY ARTIST

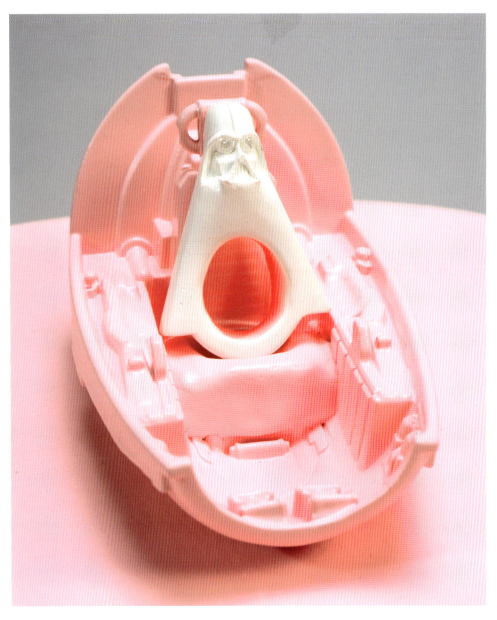

MÄRTA MATTSSON
White Vader ■ 2007
5 x 4 x 2 cm
Resin, cubic zirconias, plastic
PHOTO BY ARTIST

JENNIFER MALLEY
Trekkie ■ 2009

10.2 x 2.5 x 2.5 cm
Sterling silver; fabricated
PHOTO BY RICHARD NICOL

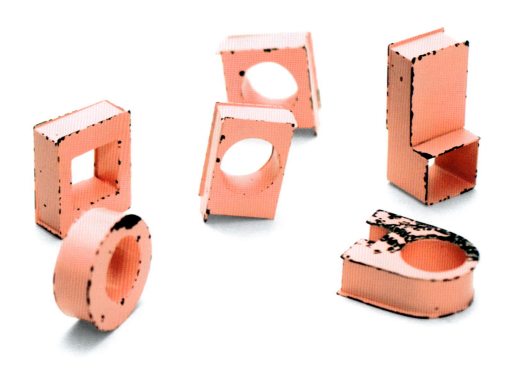

SARA BORGEGÅRD
From the Home Collection: Pink Rings ◼ 2010
Each: 3.5 x 2.5 x 1.5 cm
Iron, lacquer paint; soldered, painted
PHOTO BY ARTIST

AMI AVELLÁN
Puffball ■ 2011

11.5 x 7.8 x 2.5 cm
Handmade reindeer skin, bone pearls,
sewing thread, synthetic pillow filling
PHOTO BY ARTIST

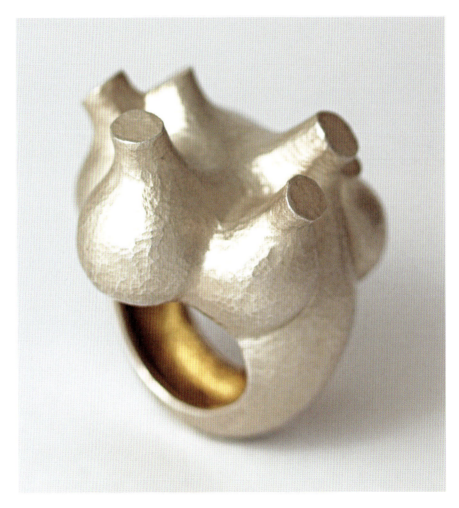

TSUBA MURAYAMA
Growth I ■ 2011

3.5 x 3 x 3.2 cm
Pure silver, 24-karat gold leaf
PHOTO BY ARTIST

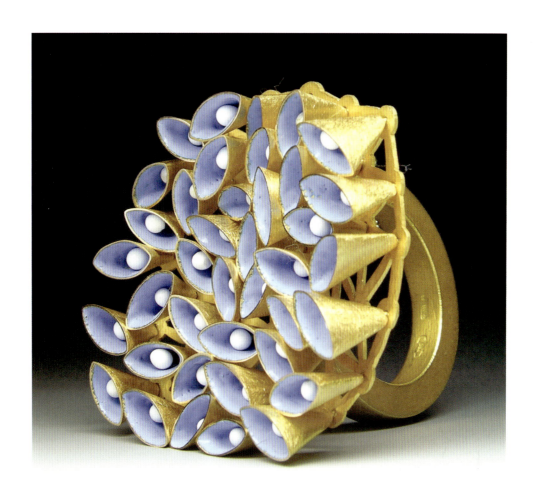

JACQUELINE RYAN
Ring with Moveable Elements ■ 2008
3.5 x 3.5 x 3.5 cm
18-karat gold, glass enamel
PHOTO BY ARTIST

DIANA VINCENT
Dancing Twizzle: Blue Topaz ■ 2002

2.5 cm wide
Sterling silver, yellow gold, blue topaz; polished
PHOTO BY SIMON JUTRAS

AMY RENSHAW
Left: *My Friend + I—Rubies;*
Right: *My Friend + I—Sapphires* ■ 2010

Each: 2 x 0.5 cm
18-karat matte yellow gold, rubies, Ceylon
sapphires, diamonds; handmade, set
PHOTOS BY TERENCE BOGUE

ELENA THIVEOU
Ecosphere ■ 2010
3.9 x 2 x 1.8 cm
Sterling silver, 18-karat gold, chrysoprase;
forged, hollow-form constructed, oxidized
PHOTO BY ALEXANDER CROWE

PETRA CLASS

Untitled ■ 2009

2.5 x 2.5 x 2.5 cm
18-karat gold, 22-karat gold, green
tourmaline, diamond; fabricated
PHOTO BY HAP SAKWA

SEOHEE KOH

Two Rings ■ 2003

Largest: 3.4 x 2.5 x 1.7 cm
18-karat gold, custom-cut crystal and
rutile crystal cubes; scored, fabricated

Made from special alloys, this ring consists of 104,272 small, single wires. When caressed, the soft, fur-like surface of the piece provides an amazing and pleasurable tactile experience. —GC

GIOVANNI CORVAJA
From the Golden Fleece Collection: Fidelity ■ 2008
2.4 x 1.8 x 1.6 cm
18-karat gold; hand-drawn wire, constructed
PHOTO BY ARTIST

TOM MUNSTEINER
Hexagon ■ 2010

3.2 x 2.5 cm
Green tourmaline, red tourmaline,
18-karat yellow gold
PHOTO BY LICHTBLICK/CULLMANN

VANESSA SAMUELS
Thira and Samaria Gorge #1 ▪ 2010

Various dimensions
Sterling silver, 18-karat gold,
rhodium finish; hollow constructed
PHOTO BY JOHN LEE

SOPHIE HANAGARTH
Forged Balls Ring ■ 2009
7 x 2.5 x 1.2 cm
Iron; forged
PHOTO BY ENRICO BARTOLUCCI

TAISUKE NAKADA
Being ■ 2003
6.3 x 6 x 3.1 cm
Iron, 24-karat gold leaf; cut, inlaid
PHOTO BY ARTIST

ALIKI APOUSSIDOU
Kreisquadrat ■ 2008

1.2 x 2.2 x 2.2 cm
Mild steel; hot forged
PHOTO BY ARTIST

These rings are a series of intricately crafted porcelain pieces that explore ecological issues such as deforestation, abandonment, and the passage of time. Each individually constructed ring acts as a ghost-like symbol for what once was. —AVB

ANNEKE VAN BOMMEL
Stump Ring Series ■ 2010

Various dimension
Porcelain; hand buil
PHOTO BY ARTIS

SOFIE DE BAKKER
Untitled ■ 2010

4 x 2 x 0.5 cm
Polyester, ossa sepia; cast, burned
PHOTOS BY ARTIST

DINA GONZALEZ MASCARO
Hidden Building ■ 2010
3.5 x 3 x 2.5 cm
Sterling silver; oxidized
PHOTO BY SHANNON MENDES

ANGELA BUBASH
Fin #5 ■ 2010
2.5 x 4.5 x 3 cm
Sterling silver, glass, dyed feathers;
fabricated, oxidized
PHOTOS BY JONATHAN HELLER

MARGARITA SAMPSON
Suture ■ 2011
6 x 4 x 4 cm
Sterling silver, golf ball, linen
thread; fabricated, oxidized
PHOTO BY ROBIN NISBETT

JANA BREVICK
Relay Ring ■ 2009

5.5 x 3 x 3 cm
Nixie tube, sterling silver; fabricated
PHOTO BY DOUG YAPLE

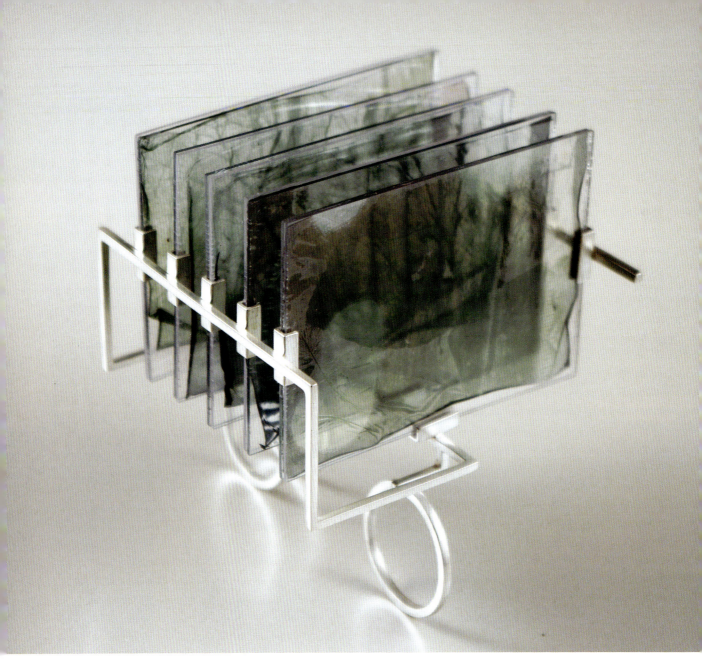

GRACE M. GAYNOR
Woods ■ 2011
7 x 6.5 x 6 cm
Sterling silver, clear plastic sheeting,
film; fabricated, manipulated
PHOTO BY ARTIST

NIYATI FROIND
Saltwater Ring ■ 2011
3.9 x 2.5 x 1.9 cm
Sterling silver, rough
aquamarine; forged, oxidized
PHOTO BY YARON WEINBERG

I find great inspiration in antique buttons and embrace the challenge of showcasing their natural beauty. Once ordinary and common, these timeless "gems" of history come to rest in my hands after decades of functional use. It's my goal to breathe new life into them. —NS

NISA SMILEY
Collection of Antique Shell Button Rings ■ 2010
Various dimensions
Sterling silver, 24-karat gold leaf, green tourmalines, prehnite, antique shell buttons; hand fabricated, forged, bezel set, stamped, keum boo
PHOTO BY ROBERT DIAMANTE

DYLAN JOHNSON
Perched Gargoyle ■ 2011
7.6 x 2.5 x 3.2 cm
White bronze, citrine;
carved, lost wax cast
PHOTO BY YUKO YAGISAWA

HATTIE SANDERSON
Untitled ■ 2010
5.5 x 3.5 x 3.5 cm
Fine silver, lampworked bead,
steel nuts and bolts
PHOTO BY ARTIST

RACHEL KEDINGER
Turned Corners ■ 2009

7.6 x 5.1 cm
Brass corner protectors, sterling
silver, powder coat; formed

PHOTO BY FRANKIE FLOOD

ALLYSON GEE

8 Satyrinae ■ 2010

10 x 10 x 4 cm
Satyrinae butterflies,
steel; laser welded
PHOTO BY SOPHIE DYER

MARCUS I. SYNNOT
Subtle Warm Heart ■ 2011

3.8 x 3.8 x 3.8 cm
Fine silver, sterling silver,
18-karat gold; keum boo
PHOTO BY MATT REED

NATALIE ISAAK KNOTT
About to Leap ■ 2010

3 x 2 x 1.8 cm
Fine silver metal clay; formed,
carved, fired, keum boo, oxidized
PHOTO BY GEORGE POST

NATALIE ISAAK KNOTT
Gasping ■ 2010

2.5 x 2 x 2 cm
Fine silver metal clay; formed,
carved, fired, brushed
PHOTO BY GEORGE POST

303

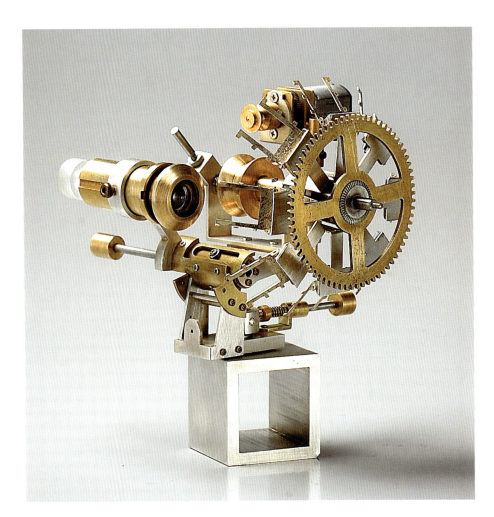

MANKI KOH
Analog + Digital—Kinetic ■ 2010
9 x 6 x 7 cm
Sterling silver, brass, steel, spring,
motor, bearing, LED; hand fabricated
PHOTO BY STUDIO MUNCH

KRISTIN DIENER
Ring Form: Contraption ■ 2008

15.5 x 5.5 x 1 cm
Sterling silver, fine silver, brass, bone toothpick, plastic toys and charms,
antique drapery parts, dog tooth; handmade bezel, prong, and contraption set,
hollow-form torch fabricated, sawed, pierced, oxidized, burnished, hand finished

MOLLY HUNT MCKINLEY
The Wedding Ring and The Affair Ring ■ 2010

2.3 x 2 x 1 cm
Sterling silver, cubic zirconia,
black flocking; fabricated
PHOTOS BY ARTIST

KENNETH C. MACBAIN
All Mine Forever ■ 2010
2.5 x 3.8 x 2.5 cm
Steel, cubic zirconias; lathe turned,
prong set, tap-and-die threaded
PHOTO BY ARTIST

307

MI-MI MOSCOW

From the Frog Can Fly Series: Siberian Postman ■ 2005

17.5 x 7 x 7 cm

Frog, melhior, acrylic, coloring

PHOTO BY ARTIST

ELLIOT GASKIN
Silver Machine ■ 2009
15.2 x 10.2 x 10.2 cm
Sterling silver, wood, string
PHOTO BY IAN MCNEMAR

NILS SCHMALENBACH
A Space ■ 2008
3.5 x 1.5 x 2 cm
Sterling silver; printed
PHOTO BY ARTIST

KELLIE RIGGS
Pyrite Growth Ring ■ 2009
4 x 2.5 x 6 cm
Brass; wire constructed, hollow constructed
PHOTO BY ANNICK THOMAS

In designing *Big Fish*, I wanted to create a piece that reflected the unpredictable and adaptable natures of the lives of international students living in the United States. I placed the bobbers in a fish tank filled with water and kept them moving with a motor. The rings come in 30 different sizes. —BC

BIFEI CAO
Big Fish ■ 2009

Various dimensions
Sterling silver, fish bobbers, decal paper,
fish tank, air pump; printed, varnished
PHOTO BY ARTIST

SAKURAKO SHIMIZU
"I Do" Wedding Bands ▨ 2008
Largest: 0.8 x 2.2 cm
18-karat yellow gold, palladium; laser cut, fabricated
PHOTO BY TAKATERU YAMADA

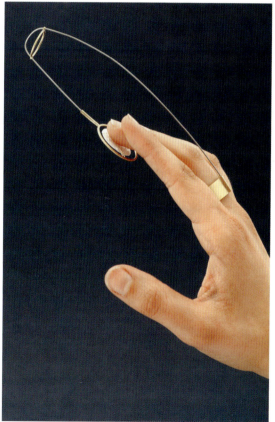

GALIT BARAK
Text(ure) Ring ■ 2011
13.5 x 5.5 x 2.8 cm
Brass, steel, paper; soldered, fabricated
PHOTOS BY SHENKAR COLLEGE OF ENGINEERING AND DESIGN

CHRISTY KLUG
Graphite Ring ■ 2009

4 x 4 x 1 cm
Enamel, 18-karat gold, silver, graphite,
copper; oxidized, fabricated
PHOTO BY HAP SAKWA

VERENA SCHREPPEL
Take and Give—Africa Ring ■ 2010
3 x 2.9 x 3.1 cm
Maple; hand sawed
PHOTO BY ARTIST

MYUNGJOO LEE
Recollection ■ 2011
4 x 8.5 x 2 cm
Sterling silver, jangpan-ji; formed, oxidized
PHOTO BY MYUNG-WOOK HUH

315

DOMINIQUE LABORDERY
Breaking through Barriers ■ 2008

5 cm
Fine silver
PHOTO BY MARTIN W. MAIER

KEVIN PHAUP
Untitled ■ 2011

Band: 2.5 x 2.5 x 1 cm
Sterling silver, brass, rubber; cast
PHOTO BY SCOTT KISSELL

317

I use text in my jewelry in order to communicate with my audience in a direct manner. With these rings, the wearer can make his own statement. They may be worn individually or as part of a group to form words or phrases. Each ring is 0.2 cm thick, making it possible to wear 10 or more at a time. —TH

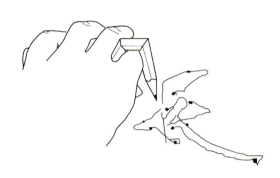

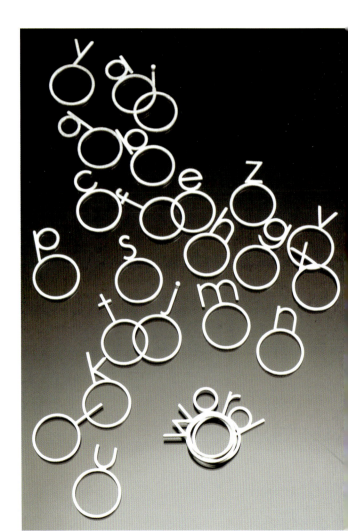

NICOLAS CHENG
Untitled ■ 2010
0.8 x 5 x 4 cm
Wood, graphite, gold paint
PHOTOS BY ARTIST

TRUDEE HILL
Letters from Words: Alphabet Rings ■ 2010
Each: 3.8 x 2.2 x 0.2 cm
Sterling silver; fabricated
PHOTO BY DOUG YAPLE

Showcase 500
rings

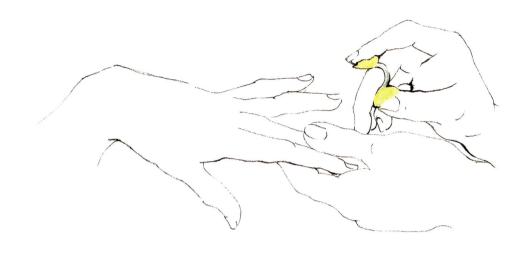

JOOHYUN LEE
Conscious Pressure ■ 2008
3 x 2 x 2 cm
18-karat gold, sterling silver
PHOTOS BY STUDIO MUNCH

MIREK GOMOLKA
Suntares ▪ 2007

3 x 2 x 2.8 cm
Titanium, silver, ruby, 24-karat gold, copper,
epoxy plastic resin; hand fabricated, cast
PHOTO BY ARTIST

I drew inspiration for this ring while watching two birds construct their nest. The ring incorporates various materials, including copper, brass, wood, seed, and sandstone, to create a natural nest for the finger of the wearer. —AS

ADAR SIDAHI
The Nest ■ 2009
7 x 5.8 x 1.3 cm
Copper, brass, wood fibers, metal, sterling silver, natural seed, sandstone; entwined
PHOTO BY ROY MIZRACHI

In creating this piece, I wanted to provide the viewer with an experience reminiscent of reading and leafing, where the printed word would produce a pattern. Staying true to the source of inspiration, I fabricated the key elements from old book paper and covers. The materials used thus embody the story held within. —SA

SHIRI AVDA
Sea of Tranquility ■ 2010
6.5 x 6 x 8 cm
Sterling silver, book paper, ink; hand fabricated
PHOTOS BY TAL SCHIFFMAN

KENTA KATAKURA
Naked ■ 2010
8 x 6 x 8 cm
Wood; shaved, bonded
PHOTO BY TAKAYUKI SERI

323

LAURA PRIETO-VELASCO
Chupacabra 3 ■ 2010
12.7 x 5.1 x 5.1 cm
Steel, latex paint, gold-plated
silver; fabricated, airbrushed
PHOTO BY ARTIST

DANIEL COOK
Alchemist's Ring ■ 2009

5 cm in diameter
Lead, 24-karat gold; cast, electroplated
PHOTO BY ARTIST

ULRIKE KLEINE-BEHNKE
Sprout 1 ▥ 2010
4 x 2.5 x 3 cm
Silver; cast, oxidized
PHOTO BY ARTIST

ULRIKE KLEINE-BEHNKE
Red Sprout ▥ 2010
5 x 3.5 x 2 cm
Silver, patina; cast
PHOTO BY ARTIST

MEL MILLER
Mnemochronology, No. 4
(Object with Removable Rings) ■ 2009

20 x 19 x 12 cm
Fine silver, enamel, fabric, wool;
fused, repoussé, felted, sewn

327

In the *Worshipper* series, I investigate the female universe—its ambiguities and inherent contradictions—through a contrast of techniques: readymade forms and laser-cut components versus handmade lines created with thread and paint. I chose porcelain and fabric because they're traditionally associated with the feminine. —MF

MIRLA FERNANDES
From the Worshipper Series: Silence ■ 2010
2 x 10 x 2 cm
Porcelain, fabric, threads;
laser cut, sewn, painted
PHOTO BY BIANCA VIANI

TOP
MIRLA FERNANDES
*From the Worshipper Series:
I Touched Slightly* ■ 2010

4 x 3 x 3 cm
Porcelain, fabric, threads;
laser cut, sewn, painted
PHOTO BY BIANCA VIANI

GABRIELA HORVAT
Inner Parts ■ 2010
7 x 4 x 2 cm
Sterling silver, silk, wool; coiled, soldered
PHOTO BY ARTIST

JOHANNA DAHM
Clay ■ 2008
4.1 x 2.5 x 1.6 cm
22-karat gold, steel, rough yellow diamonds
PHOTO BY REINHARD ZIMMERMANN

JESS STARKEL
Zest Ring ■ 2005

2 x 2 x 2 cm
Polyurethane rubber, citrine; cast
PHOTO BY ARTIST

JACK GUALTIERI, ZAFFIRO
Untitled ■ 2008
3.5 x 3.1 x 2.2 cm
22-karat gold, 18-karat gold, mandarin garnet,
diamonds; fused, granulation, bezel and flush set
PHOTO BY DANIEL VAN ROSSEN

Showcase 500
rings

CECELIA BAUER
Signature Ring ■ 2008
3 x 2.2 x 1.4 cm
22-karat gold, spessartite garnet;
granulation, fabricated
PHOTO BY RALPH GABRINER

BARBARA HEINRICH
Multi-Wrapped Gold Ring with Diamonds ■ 2010
1.2 x 2.2 x 2.3 cm
18-karat yellow gold, diamonds; hand fabricated, formed
PHOTO BY TIM CALLAHAN

STUART GOLDER

Patchwork Dazzle ■ 2009

2.5 x 2.5 x 1.3 cm
18-karat pink, white, yellow, and green gold,
pink sapphires, spinels, diamonds
PHOTO BY ARTIST

SHINLYOUNG KIM
Ring 1 ■ 2008
2.2 x 3.5 x 0.7 cm
Sterling silver, nickel silver; marriage of metal
PHOTOS BY KYUNGHEE JUNG

This ring was inspired by the concepts of movement and fluidity. Each carefully engineered piece consists of a three-dimensional geometric shape. When worn, the design creates an illusion of perpetual movement. —MK

MOMOKO KUMAI
Untitled ■ 2007
1 x 2.3 x 2.3 cm
Silver; soldered
PHOTO BY REINA SENGA

EMANUELA DUCA
Magma Rings ■ 2010
Largest: 2 x 2 x 3 cm
Sterling silver, diamonds;
oxidized, wax sculpted
PHOTO BY RON BOSZKO

JEE HYE KWON
Butterfly ■ 2008

7 x 6 x 6 cm
Sterling silver, 24-karat gold, copper, black
diamonds; shakudo, marriage of metal
PHOTO BY RALPH GABRINER

KENTA KATAKURA
Naked ■ 2010
6 x 5 x 8 cm
Wood; shaved, bonded
PHOTO BY TAKAYUKI SERI

JULIAN PASTORINO
CECILIA SUAREZ
From the Fragmentos Collection: Geyser ■ 2010
3 x 2.5 x 2 cm
Resin; cast, sandblasted
PHOTO BY SIMONE BARBERIS

SERIN OH

Imitation & Deception ■ 2011

5.5 x 6.6 x 6 cm
Sterling silver, 24-karat gold/
ruthenium plating; wax cast

STEPHANIE JENDIS

Matterhorn ■ 2005

5.5 x 3.5 x 2 cm
Ebony, 18-karat gold, synthetic stone

Showcase 500
rings

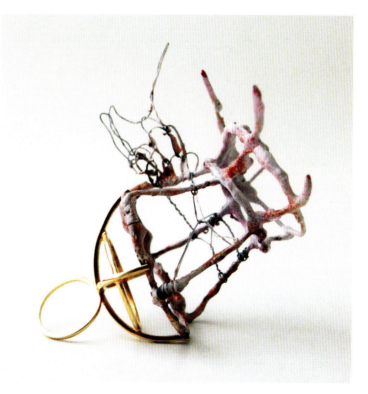

LAURA PRIETO-VELASCO
Chupacabra 2 ■ 2010
12.7 x 5.1 x 5.1 cm
Steel, latex paint, gold-plated
silver; fabricated, airbrushed
PHOTOS BY ARTIST

343

SEAN O'CONNELL
Knuckleduster Ballrings ■ 2006
Each: 3.2 x 3.2 x 0.7 cm
9-karat rose gold, sterling silver, industrial
ball bearings; cast, fabricated, riveted
PHOTO BY ALBERT PACA

JORGE GIL
Arches I ■ 2009
3.5 x 4.8 x 1.3 cm
Titanium; forged, chiseled
heat colored, tension set
PHOTO BY RAUL CASAS ANCA

KATIE SCHUTTE
White Ring ■ 2009

9 x 9 x 7 cm
Found wire, copper, plastic, cubic zirconia;
crocheted, fabricated, electroformed, powder coated
PHOTO BY JEFF SABO

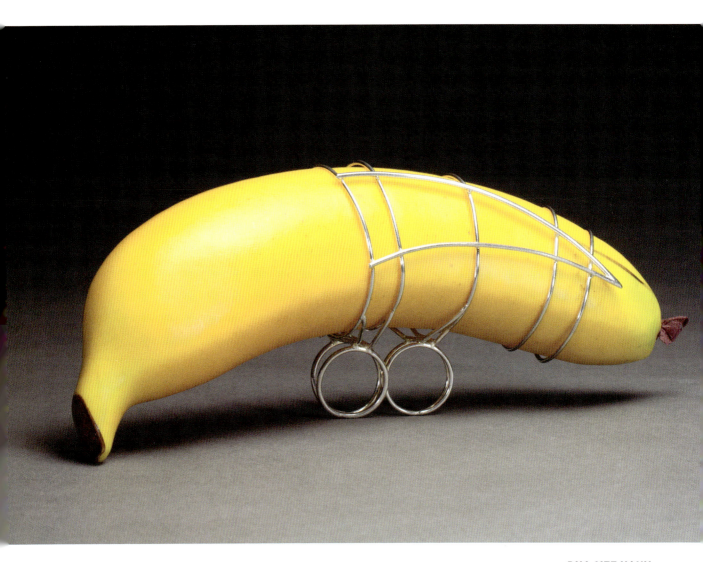

DHA-MEE HAHN
Banana Gun Ring ■ 2010
7 x 20 x 4 cm
Sterling silver, artificial
banana; friction fit
PHOTO BY ARTIST

Inheritance celebrates the pride men take in their innate ability to continue their bloodlines. The scale of the ring very blatantly supports this concept. I find it fascinating that something so small can carry so much power and information. —AV

ARIC VERRASTRO
Inheritance ■ 2011
2.3 x 0.5 x 0.3 m
Fabric, plastic balls, copper, patina,
sterling silver, lapis lazuli; hand dyed
PHOTO BY BRUCE FOX

MALENE KASTALJE
Did It Grow Like That! ■ 2010
18.8 x 8.6 x 5.7 cm
Silicone rubber, pigment, cotton, nylon,
wood, silver; embroidered, cast
PHOTO BY ARTIST

I use recognizable, everyday items to create conceptual objects for the human body—vast and conspicuous pieces of jewelry that truly come to life when worn. My purpose in designing this ring was to challenge the limits of size and usability. —CP

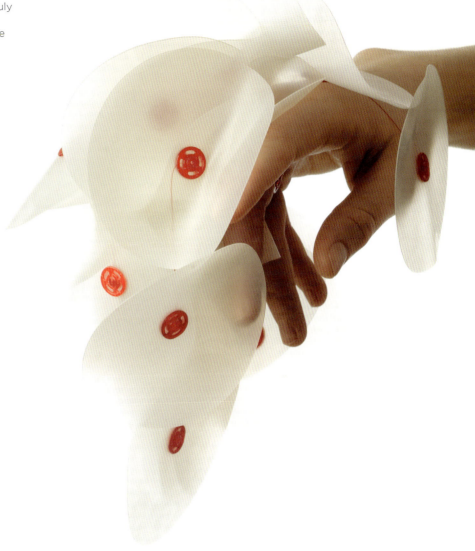

CAMILLA PRASCH
Mega ■ 2009

11 x 31 cm
Snap fasteners, nylon thread,
silicone discs; dyed, cut, sewn
PHOTOS BY DORTE KROGH

349

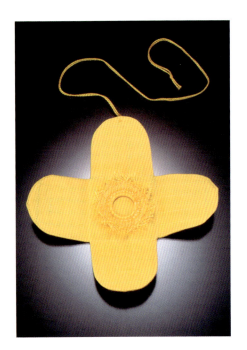

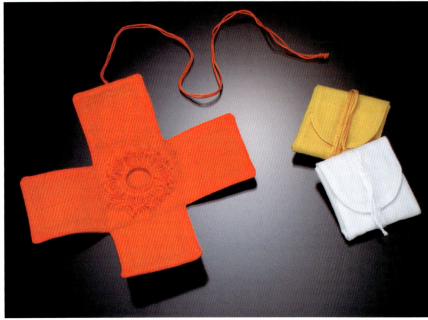

MEGAN DUNN
Mandala Series ■ 2005

Each: 15.5 x 15.5 x 0.3 cm
Sterling silver, cotton, thread; machine stitched,
hand woven, fabricated, hand dyed
PHOTOS BY ROBERT DIAMANTE

GILL FORSBROOK
Untitled ■ 2009

2 x 2.8 x 2.8 cm
Polypropylene, aluminum, silver; hand fabricated
PHOTO BY ARTIST

RUBY AITCHISON
Pumpking ▦ 2011
8.5 x 5 x 6 cm
Pumpkin, sterling silver; blackened
PHOTO BY ARTIST

SHELBY FERRIS FITZPATRICK
Edible Sociable Rings ■ 2001
Empty: 3 x 4.4 x 4.4 cm each; filled: 5 x 4.4 x 4.4 cm each
Sterling silver, 24-karat gold plate, dried edible food; spun, fabricated
PHOTOS BY MIKE BLISSETT

EMMA GERARD
Separation ■ 2011
2 x 2.5 x 3 cm
Glass; flameworked

NATALIA MILOSZ-PIEKARSKA
Garlic Ring ■ 2010
3 x 3 x 3 cm
Sterling silver, timber, paint;
oxidized, lost wax cast, carved

SARAH HOOD
Landscape Sample Rings ■ 2007

Each: 5 x 3.8 x 1.3 cm
Sterling silver, model railroad
landscape materials; fabricated
PHOTO BY DOUG YAPLE

JEFFREY LLOYD DEVER
Convergence ■ 2011
7.6 x 7 x 2.5 cm
Polymer clay, steel, cardstock;
fabricated, sculpted
PHOTO BY GREGORY R. STALEY

YOUNJI CHOI
Squeezed Ring ■ 2010
5 x 6 x 4 cm
Photopolymers; dyed, 3D printed
PHOTO BY MYUNG WOOK HUH

HANNAH CARLYLE
Boulder Ring ■ 2010
5.5 x 4 x 4 cm
Sterling silver, hand-pigmented resin
PHOTO BY KARA GROWDEN

FABRIZIO TRIDENTI
Restricted Area ■ 2010

5.8 x 4.3 x 3.4 cm
Brass, acrylic paint; constructed
PHOTO BY ARTIST

STEFANO MARCHETTI
Untitled ■ 2004
4 x 3.5 x 3.5 cm
18-karat gold
PHOTO BY ARTIST

JACQUELINE RYAN
Ring with Moveable Segments ■ 2009

1.6 cm wide
18-karat gold, glass enamel
PHOTO BY ARTIST

MARCIA HELMAN
Sunflowers ■ 2011
2.5 x 3 x 3.5 cm
Sterling silver, recycled silicon keyboard
pieces; hand fabricated, riveted
PHOTO BY STELLA RUBIO

MARJORIE SCHICK
The Ring That Got Out of Hand ■ 2004

Hand sculpture: 23.2 x 28.6 x 19.1 cm; base: 5.4 x 29.6 x 29.6 cm
Wood, plastic laminate, bronze; constructed, glued, painted, riveted
PHOTO BY GARY POLLMILLER

GIOVANNI SICURO 'MINTO'
Untitled ■ 2010
4.2 x 3.6 x 2.1 cm
Silver, niello; hollow constructed
PHOTO BY ARTIST

SAND-DEOK HAN

Body 2 ■ 2011

Each: 2.5 x 2.9 x 2 cm
Iron; soldered, oxidized, painted, sawn
PHOTO BY ARTIST

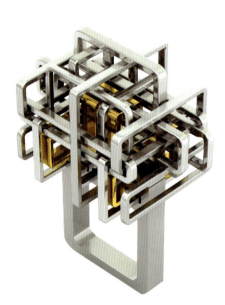

EVELYN K. HUANG
Squared ■ 2010

4.1 x 3.5 x 3.3 cm
Sterling silver, 18-karat yellow gold;
cast, polished, laser soldered
PHOTO BY YU-HSIANG MICHAEL HUANG

SIMON HARRISON
Caddis Cascade Ring ■ 2009

3.3 x 3.3 x 1.3 cm
Rhodium plate, Swarovski crystal
PHOTO BY NEIL SPENCE

MARY HALLAM PEARSE
For Pleasure . . . or Marriage ■ 2009

17 x 10.5 x 1.5 cm
Paperboard, linen, fabric, flocking, sterling silver, cubic
zirconia; traditional box-making techniques, fabricated
PHOTO BY ARTIST

KATIE SCHUTTE
Blue Ring ■ 2009

6 x 4.5 x 5 cm
Found wire, copper, plastic, cubic zirconia;
crocheted, fabricated, electroformed, powder coated
PHOTO BY JEFF SABO

EVELYN SILVA
Candy ■ 2011

Each: 4 x 2 x 2 cm
Cork, silver
PHOTOS BY PEDRO SEQUEIRA

KIMBERLY VOIGT
A Ring a Day: July 2008 ■ 2008
Various dimensions
Sterling silver, gypsum, pigment,
24-karat gold leaf; 3D printed, cast
PHOTO BY ARTIST

LIMOR LESHINSKER
Untitled ▦ 2010
3 x 2.8 x 2 cm
Sterling silver, adhesive tape, zircon
PHOTO BY RAANAN COHEN

SANDRINE VIEIRA
Suction Ring ■ 2009
8 x 6 x 2 cm
Silver, suction cup
PHOTOS BY ARTIST

KATHERINE RUDOLPH
Mirrored Illusion ■ 2009
2.6 x 2.6 x 2.6 cm
Sterling silver, clear plastic
sheeting; constructed
PHOTO BY DEAN POWELL

SARAH KING
Untitled ■ 2001

Each: 3 x 2.6 x 1.3 cm
Bioresin, sterling silver; cast
PHOTO BY JEREMY JOHNS PHOTOGRAPHY

SANNA SVEDESTEDT
Birch Diamond/Snow ■ 2010
5 x 3 x 1.5 cm
Wood, lacquer
PHOTO BY ARTIST

CLAUDIA COSTA
Untitled ▪ 2011

Each: 3 x 2.4 x 1 cm
Resin, pigment, topaz; cast
PHOTO BY ARTIST

GAYLE EASTMAN
Moss Pool ■ 2009

2.8 x 2.2 x 3.8 cm
18-karat gold, 22-karat gold,
tourmaline; forged, fabricated
PHOTO BY HAP SAKWA

KOL S. NAYLOR
Nature Series 300 | 2011

4 x 2.5 x 2 cm
24-karat gold, 22-karat gold,
18-karat gold; cast, fabricated
PHOTO BY ARTIST

JULIE LYNN ROMANENKO
Untitled ▪ 2010
Each: 3 x 2 x 0.1 cm
14-karat gold; cast, hand set
PHOTO BY MARILYN O'HARA

CHI HUYNH OF GALATEU
Dignity ■ 2010
2.8 x 2.5 x 1 cm
14-karat yellow gold, white
diamonds, white topaz; cast, cut
PHOTO BY HAP SAKWA

YOUNGJOO YOO
The Laurel Blossom ■ 2010
5.5 x 5 x 4 cm
18-karat gold and sterling silver bimetal,
sterling silver; hand cut, fabricated, soldered
PHOTO BY STUDIO MUNCH

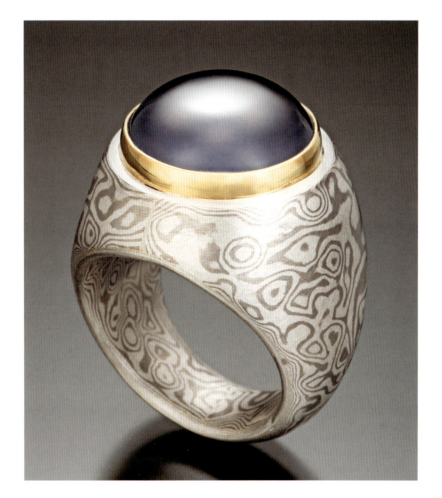

CHRIS PLOOF
Mokume Gane Hollow-Construction
Ring with Chalcedony ■ 2010

3 x 2.3 x 2.1 cm
14-karat palladium white gold, silver, 18-karat yellow
gold; mokume gane, forged, fabricated
PHOTO BY ROBERT DIAMANTE

383

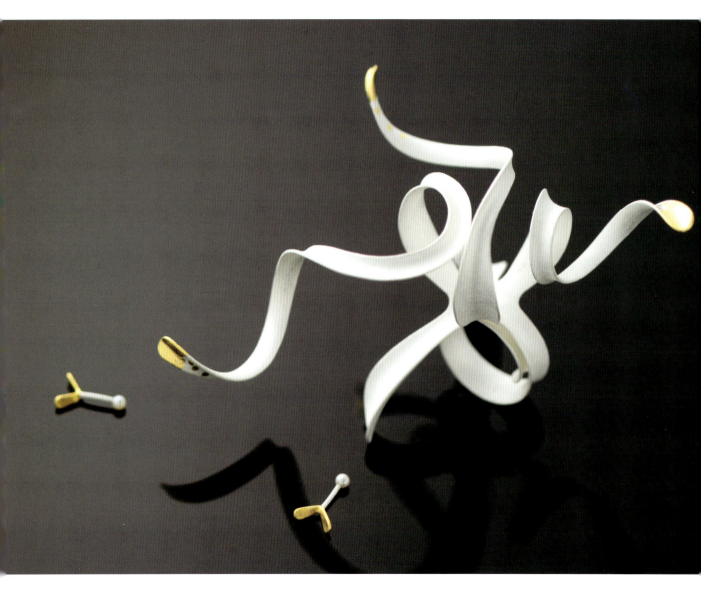

CHAO-HSIEN KUO
Spotty Sunshine—Where to ■ 2010
6 x 6 x 11 cm
Sterling silver, 24-karat gold foil, pearls;
anticlastic forming, keum boo
PHOTO BY ARTIST

VINA RUST
Ring #2: Stamen Series ■ 2004
5.6 x 5 x 0.3 cm
Sterling silver, 22-karat gold, liver of
sulfur patina; hand fabricated
PHOTO BY DOUG YAPLE

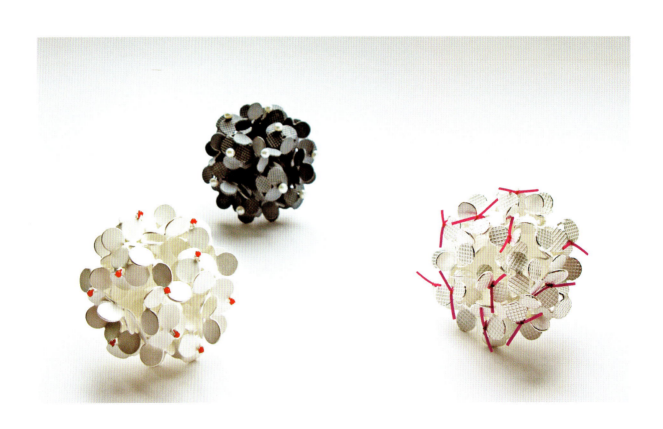

MISUN WON
Hydrangeas ▩ 2008
Each: 4.8 x 4.8 x 5 cm
Sterling silver, coral, pearl, elastic
string; fabricated, etched, oxidized
PHOTO BY ARTIST

SIAN ELIZABETH HUGHES
Foliage Ring ■ 2011
3.5 x 2 x 0.5 cm
Sterling silver, silver;
oxidized, folded, textured
PHOTO BY J. HYTCH

NATALIE ISAAK KNOTT
Barn Owl ▧ 2010
3.3 x 2.2 x 2 cm
Fine silver metal clay;
formed, carved, fired
PHOTO BY GEORGE POST

RUI KIKUCHI
PLAnta Ring (Yellow and Green) ▧ 2009
5 x 7.5 cm
Bottle, silver; hand cut, hand
dyed, riveted, fabricated
PHOTO BY ARTIST

LEEJUNG KIM
Dancing Flower ■ 2009
Largest: 5 x 5.5 x 3 cm
Sterling silver; oxidized
PHOTO BY KC STUDIO

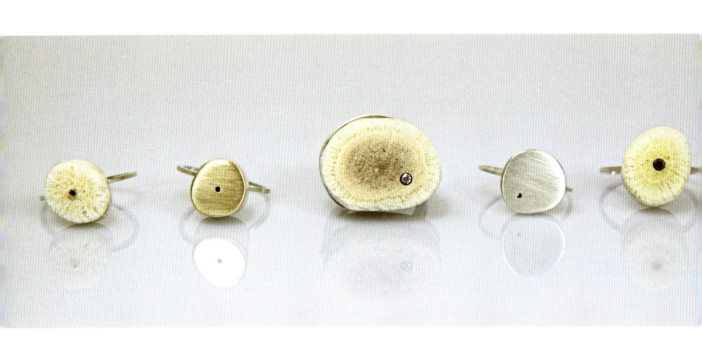

ARAM MOON
Blooming Ocean ■ 2011
Various dimensions
Sterling silver, fine silver, brass, natural sponge,
cubic zirconia; fabricated, oxidized, set
PHOTO BY ARTIST

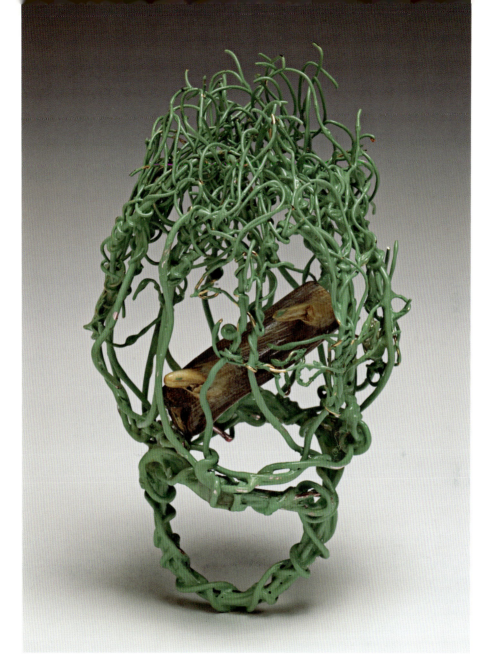

SHARONA MUIR
Prairie Grass Ring ■ 2009
7.5 x 4.5 x 4 cm
Mixed media, blue coral, polychrome
PHOTO BY TOM MUIR

KARI RINN
Elemental ■ 2006
4 x 7 x 1 cm
Sterling silver, organic
material; constructed
PHOTOS BY TAYLOR DABNEY

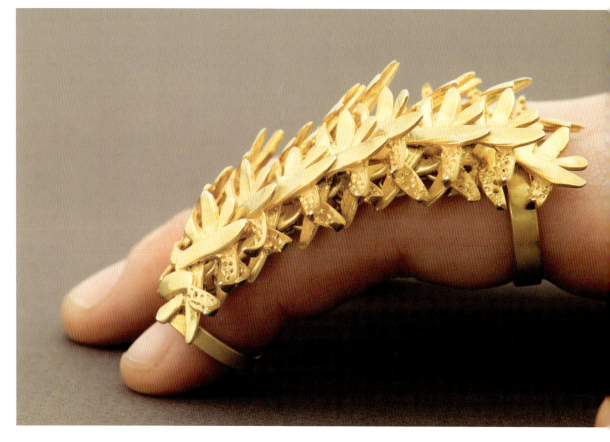

LIOR SHULAK
Untitled ■ 2010
6.5 x 4 x 2 cm
24-karat gold plate, brass; cast
PHOTO BY AMOS TRABULSKY

LITAL MENDEL
(precious) Stones ■ 2008
Largest: 6 x 5 x 2 cm
Brass, stone, plastic, zirconia;
vacuum formed
PHOTO BY NOA KEDMI

ALLYSON GEE
3 Chinese Nawab ■ 2010

7 x 3.5 x 3 cm
Chinese Nawab butterflies,
steel; laser welded
PHOTO BY SOPHIE DYER

This ring explores themes of growth, transformation, and disintegration. It combines permanent materials—textiles—with a temporary substance—sugar. The combination provides the ring with a constantly changing structure. Once the design was completed, the piece began its transitory existence. **—NS**

NATALIE SMITH
Rushing to Paradise ■ 2010
8 x 9 x 7.5 cm
Plastic, textiles, steel, sugar
PHOTO BY ARTIST

RUI KIKUCHI
PLAnta Ring (Red and Green) ■ 2009

10 x 5 cm
Bottle, silver; hand cut, hand
dyed, riveted, fabricated
PHOTO BY ARTIST

JILLIAN PALONE
Pseudopods ▪ 2010
Largest: 9.5 x 5 x 7.6 cm
Paper clay, paint, colored pencils; hand built
PHOTO BY ANNIE PENNINGTON

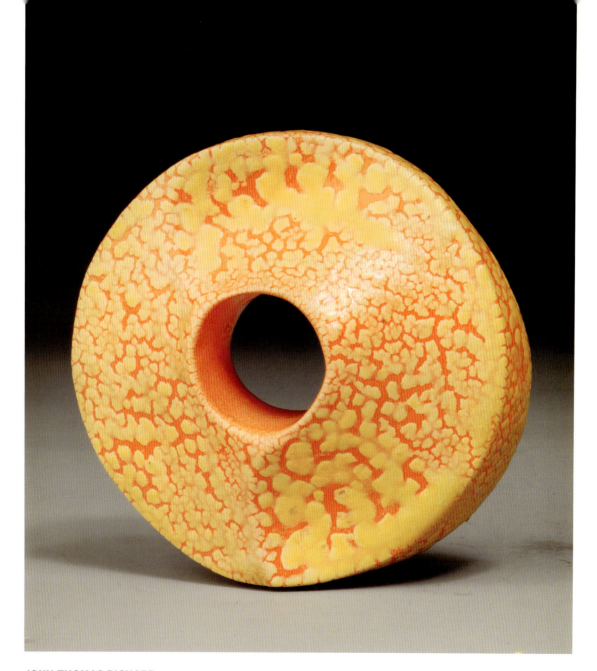

JOHN-THOMAS RICHARD
Untitled ■ 2011
7.3 x 2.5 x 7.3 cm
Ceramic, underglaze, low-fire glaze
PHOTO BY ROBLY GLOVER

This is a small-scale installation of wearable porcelain Petri dishes and rings based on the patterns, colors, and textures of bacteria. They straddle the line between the beautiful and the grotesque. —KS

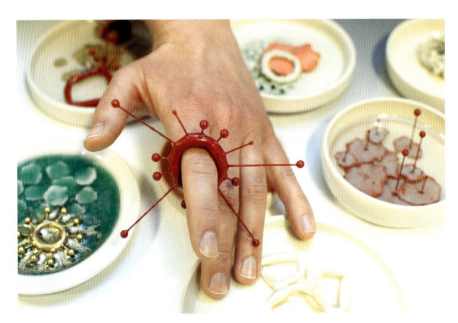

KERI STRAKA
Bacteria Rings ■ 2011

With Petri dishes: 4 x 36 x 20 cm
Porcelain clay, metal pins, thread, resin; oxidation fired, cone 6
PHOTOS BY JEN FRANKEL

ZHAO LI
Finding Neverland ■ 2010

8 x 4 x 3 cm
Silver, textile, medical-grade plastic
PHOTO BY AYU PEETERS

JOHN-THOMAS RICHARD
Untitled ■ 2011
7.5 x 1.3 x 7.5 cm
Ceramic, underglaze, low-fire glaze

SHARON VAIZER
my little fun ta sea ■ 2011

5 x 8 x 8 cm
Sterling silver, plastic, Swarovski
crystals; welded, inlaid
PHOTO BY HEFTSY ELGAR

403

RALPH BAKKER
Solitaire 6 ■ 2010
5 x 2.5 x 5 cm
Gold, silver, enamel, rock crystal
PHOTO BY MICHAEL ANHALT

TERHI TOLVANEN
Bleu ■ 2010
7 x 3 x 3 cm
Prasiolite, wood, paint, silver
PHOTO BY FRANCIS WILLEMSTIJN

In my work there's usually a tension between the attractive and the repulsive, the seductive and the dangerous. In this piece, the objects are graceful and elegant, yet they terminate in forms reminiscent of spines, blades, and interlocking plates of armor. They ask to be touched yet warn us to do so with caution. When people finally do touch the objects, they're surprised to find that they're not rigid or sharp. They're flexible, soft, and pleasant. —IH

IAN HENDERSON
Mussorgsky ■ 2010

8 x 5 x 3 cm
Aluminum grounding wire, synthetic rubber
insulation tubing; forged, cut, layered, heat treated
PHOTO BY TOM BLOOM

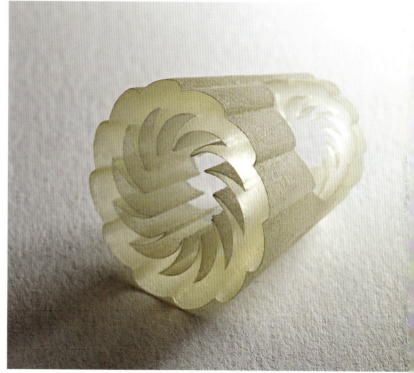

RUTI STOPNITZKI
Untitled ■ 2010
Each: 3.5 x 2.7 x 2.7 cm
Acrylic-based polymer; 3D printed
PHOTOS BY PETER GILSON

407

NATALIE SALISBURY
Bouquet Ring ■ 2010
10 x 10 x 4 cm
Brass, powder coat; hand formed
PHOTO BY DAVID WITHYCOMBE

ELA CINDORUK
Doily 2 ■ 2011
3.5 x 1.7 x 1.7 cm
Sterling silver, 18-karat gold; CNC cut,
formed, fabricated, oxidized
PHOTO BY ARTIST

MORITZ GLIK
Untitled ■ 2010
4.1 x 3.3 x 0.5 cm
18-karat yellow gold, blackened silver, rose-cut and
brilliant-cut diamonds, white sapphires; hand fabricated
PHOTO BY MARSHALL TROY

CESAR LIM
3 Multi-Gem Ball Rings ■ 2010
Each: 1.3 x 1.3 x 1.5 cm
Tourmalines, zircons, demantoids, rhodolite garnets, alexandrites, chrome
diopsides, sapphires, diamonds, silver, gold; hand forged, fabricated, oxidized
PHOTO BY VLAD LAVROVSKY

LIAUNG CHUNG YEN
Blossom Ring ▦ 2007
5 x 5 x 5 cm
18-karat gold, brown diamonds;
hand fabricated, hammered
PHOTO BY ARTIST

GABRIEL CRAIG
Untitled ■ 2009

2.5 x 2.5 x 2 cm
Recycled gold, silver, and chrome
diopside; forged, chased, fabricated
PHOTO BY ARTIST

LOREE RODKIN
Shield Ring ■ 2010
1.8 x 4.2 cm
18-karat yellow gold, black rhodium,
multi-colored diamonds
PHOTO BY JOHNA HERNANDEZ

Various ancient archaeological sites inspired this ring. It features a tiny replica of diamond-encrusted stairs leading up to pillars supporting a rare zultanite gem. —RFG

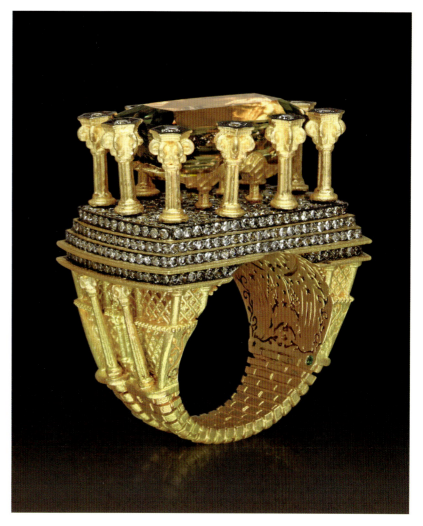

RHONDA FABER GREEN
Temple of Athena ■ 2011

3.4 x 2.9 x 2.1 cm
18-karat matte-finish yellow gold, white diamonds,
black rhodium, zultanite, green tsavorite; set
PHOTOS BY RFG DESIGNS

contributors

about the juror

Bruce Metcalf is a studio jeweler and writer from Philadelphia, Pennyslvania. He received a BFA from Syracuse University in Syracuse, New York, in 1972 and an MFA from the Tyler School of Art at Temple University in Philadelphia in 1977. He has taught at Colorado State University in Fort Collins, Colorado, the Massachusetts College of Art and Design in Boston, and the University of the Arts in Philadelphia.

Bruce's work has been included in more than 300 national and international jewelry exhibitions over the past 40 years, including *Ornament as Art: Avant-Garde Jewelry from the Helen Williams Drutt Collection*. His work is in many public collections, including the Metropolitan Museum of Art in New York City, the Renwick Gallery of the Smithsonian American Art Museum in Washington D.C., and the Montreal Museum of Fine Arts in Quebec, Canada. He has written extensively about contemporary jewelry and craft issues. With Janet Koplos, he coauthored the book *Makers: A History of American Studio Craft*.

acknowledgments

Creating jewelry books for the 500 series is a plum assignment. I've had the very good fortune to shepherd 14 of these titles from concept to call for entries to jury to store to shelf. Each book developed a character of its own during production and a life of its own once delivered to the world. Now we are back to where it all began, full circle, with a new look at rings.

I'd like to recognize two individuals who have worked on every jewelry book in the 500 series, Chris Bryant and Todd Kaderabek. Though their involvement is vital, their contributions are usually un-credited on the page and unknown outside of the office.

Chris Bryant is Lark's senior art director. He has been with Lark Crafts for 17 years. Chris is involved with the design of interiors, photography, and covers. He loves food-related titles, and he does food and photo styling for many Lark books. For *Showcase 500 Rings*, Chris designed new styles for the captions and the page layouts, and he revamped the cover. We love his updates for the series.

Todd Kaderabek is senior production manager for Lark Crafts and has been with the company 16 years. Todd is the conduit between the imprint and printer. A magician of manufacturing, he schedules, communicates, and negotiates with vendors, most of which are overseas and operate in different languages and time zones. Todd is as calm and cool as he is skillful. Without him, our books would not get made.

Many people made great contributions to this book and to others in the series. They include Carol Barnao, Dawn Dillingham, Hannah Doyle, Abby Haffelt, Julie Hale, Ray Hemachandra, Wolf Hoelscher, Kathleen Holmes, Lance Wille, Matt Shay, Shannon Yokeley, and Gavin Young. Thank you for your skill and dedication.

I feel so fortunate to have had Bruce Metcalf in the juror's seat. His insights and aesthetic set a perfect direction for this new series. Thank you for working long and hard to select such an intriguing collection.

Finally, I'd like to acknowledge the thousands of jewelers that submitted photos for this book. Your originality, imagination, and innovation make the field of jewelry truly unique. Your works are a constant source of inspiration. Thank you!

Marthe LeVan

Showcase 500 rings